Eagle-Eyed Leadership
Unleashing the Power of
31 Lessons from Eagles

Gerard Assey

Eagle-Eyed Leadership
Unleashing the Power of
31 Lessons from Eagles
By
Gerard Assey
© Copyright 2024 by Author

Published by:
Gerard Assey
19/18, Palli Arasan Street
Anna Nagar East
Chennai - 600 102

ISBN: 978-93-92492-72-3

(Image courtesy byrdyak on Freepik: 'https://www.freepik.com' Thank You)

Table of Contents

My Love for this Majestic Bird

From a very young age, I was fascinated and found myself captivated by the soaring grace and majestic presence of eagles. These remarkable birds symbolize strength, vision, and freedom, inspiring a sense of awe and wonder within me. As I grew older, my admiration for eagles deepened, and I began to recognize the profound lessons they held for leadership.

My ring has the image of an eagle, my pendant around my neck has the eagle, my office is adorned with pictures and models of eagles, my T-shirt has the picture of an eagle, my office shirts have the emblem of the eagle, my company logo and emblem is that of an eagle, my laptop and phone screens have the pictures of an eagle.

So what is it that fascinates me about this mighty bird? Their keen eyesight and ability to spot prey from great distances taught me the importance of having a clear vision as a leader. Their adaptability in navigating changing environments showed me the power of resilience and agility in the face of challenges. Their cooperative behavior within their social structure demonstrated the significance of teamwork and collaboration. These insights fueled my passion to explore further and uncover the leadership lessons embedded in the lives of these magnificent creatures.

Motivated by my love for eagles and my desire to share their wisdom, I embarked on the journey of writing a book on leadership lessons from eagles. This book seeks to illuminate the remarkable qualities and behaviors of eagles and translate them into actionable insights for leaders in the corporate world. It is a testament to my lifelong admiration for eagles and my belief in the transformative power of their teachings.

Through this book, I hope to inspire leaders to soar to new heights of excellence, embracing the principles and practices that eagles embody. May the lessons drawn from the world of eagles ignite a spark within each reader, propelling them to lead with purpose, vision, and unwavering determination.

As I share my love for eagles and the wisdom they impart, I invite you to join me on this extraordinary journey of discovering leadership lessons from these extraordinary creatures. Together, let us unlock the potential within ourselves and unleash the soaring leader within.

Preface

Welcome to **'Eagle-Eyed Leadership: Unleashing the Power of 31 Lessons from Eagles'**

In this book, we embark on a captivating journey into the world of eagles, the magnificent creatures that symbolize power, vision, and leadership. Eagles have long captivated our imaginations with their majestic flight and keen eyesight. They possess qualities that leaders can learn from and apply in their own leadership journeys.

In today's fast-paced and ever-changing corporate world, effective leadership is crucial for success. Drawing inspiration from the remarkable characteristics and behaviors of eagles, this book delves into 31 invaluable lessons that leaders can embrace to elevate their leadership skills and inspire their teams.

Each chapter explores a specific lesson, ranging from vision and focus to adaptability, strategic planning, effective communication, leading by example, coaching team members and much more. Through vivid examples, real-life case studies, and practical steps, we unravel the wisdom of eagles and demonstrate how these lessons can be translated into the corporate world.

Whether you are a seasoned leader seeking to enhance your leadership capabilities or an aspiring leader striving to make an impact, **'Eagle-Eyed Leadership'** offers a treasure trove of insights and actionable strategies. It is our hope that this book will ignite your passion for leadership, broaden your perspective, and equip you with the tools to inspire and guide others towards success.

As you immerse yourself in the pages that follow, open your mind to the teachings of eagles. Let their soaring spirit and unwavering determination propel you to new heights in your leadership journey. Embrace the lessons, apply them with intention, and witness the transformative power they can unleash.

Are you ready to soar to new horizons of leadership excellence? Let's embark on this enlightening expedition together!

Why the Eagle is considered the Most Powerful Bird, and what can Leaders Learn from it?

The eagle is considered the most powerful bird for several reasons, making it stand out among its avian counterparts. Here are some key factors that contribute to the eagle's reputation and what leaders can learn from this majestic bird:

1. Strength and Agility: The eagle possesses immense physical strength and agility, allowing it to soar at great heights, dive swiftly, and capture its prey with precision. Leaders can learn from the eagle's strength by cultivating resilience, perseverance, and the ability to navigate challenges with agility.

2. Exceptional Eyesight: Eagles have remarkable eyesight, enabling them to spot prey from vast distances. This keen vision symbolizes the importance of having a clear and far-sighted vision as a leader. By developing a clear vision, leaders can align their teams towards a common purpose and chart a course for success.

3. Fearlessness: Eagles display fearlessness in their pursuits, fearlessly taking on challenges and overcoming obstacles. Leaders can draw inspiration from the eagle's fearlessness by cultivating courage and embracing calculated risks. They must be willing to step outside their comfort zones and make bold decisions to drive innovation and growth.

4. Independence: Eagles are known for their independence and self-reliance. They are capable of hunting and surviving on their own, yet they also understand the value of working together within their social structure. Leaders can learn from the eagle's independence by developing self-confidence, autonomy, and the ability to make decisions with conviction.

5. Resilience: Eagles exhibit resilience in the face of adversity, such as harsh weather conditions or competition for resources. They adapt to changing environments and persevere in their pursuits. Leaders can learn from the eagle's resilience by embracing challenges as opportunities for growth, maintaining a positive mindset, and inspiring their teams to overcome obstacles.

6. Majestic Flight: The eagle's flight is a sight to behold, representing grace, freedom, and a sense of purpose. Leaders can learn from the eagle's flight by embracing a sense of purpose in their leadership roles, inspiring others through their actions, and creating a work environment that fosters a sense of fulfillment and empowerment.

Overall, leaders can learn from the eagle's strength, exceptional vision, fearlessness, independence, resilience, and majestic flight. By embodying these qualities, leaders can inspire their teams, navigate challenges with grace, and soar to new heights of success. The eagle serves as a powerful symbol of leadership, reminding us of the qualities and behaviors that can elevate us as leaders and drive us towards achieving our goals.

Why is it Beneficial for Leaders to Emulate and Learn these Lessons from Eagles?

Emulating and learning the lessons from eagles is beneficial and important for leaders for several reasons:

- ✓ Inspiration and Motivation: Eagles are awe-inspiring creatures that evoke a sense of wonder and admiration. By emulating their qualities and behaviors, leaders can inspire and motivate their teams. Drawing inspiration from eagles helps leaders create a compelling vision and instill a sense of purpose, driving their teams to achieve extraordinary results.
- ✓ Enhanced Leadership Skills: Learning from eagles allows leaders to develop and enhance their leadership skills. Whether it's developing a clear vision, fostering effective communication, making strategic decisions, or promoting collaboration, the lessons from eagles provide practical insights and strategies that can be applied in the corporate world.
- ✓ Adaptability in a Changing Environment: Eagles are adaptable creatures, capable of navigating changing environments and overcoming challenges. In today's rapidly changing business landscape, leaders must also be adaptable to thrive. Embracing the lessons from eagles helps leaders develop the agility and resilience necessary to navigate

uncertainty and lead their teams through change.

- ✓ Fostering a Positive Organizational Culture: Emulating the lessons from eagles helps leaders create a positive organizational culture. By demonstrating qualities such as empathy, humility, transparency, and ethical decision-making, leaders foster trust, collaboration, and a sense of belonging among team members. This contributes to a positive work environment and improves employee engagement and satisfaction.
- ✓ Driving Innovation and Growth: Eagles exhibit innovation and creativity in their hunting techniques, constantly adapting and finding new ways to capture prey. Leaders who learn from eagles can foster a culture of innovation and growth within their organizations. By encouraging new ideas, embracing calculated risks, and promoting continuous learning, leaders can drive innovation and position their organizations for sustainable growth.
- ✓ Building Resilient and High-Performing Teams: Eagles display resilience in the face of adversity, and leaders who emulate this quality can inspire their teams to do the same. By embracing resilience, leaders foster a resilient mindset within their teams, enabling them to overcome challenges, bounce back from setbacks, and maintain high performance even in demanding situations.
- ✓ Personal Growth and Development: Emulating the lessons from eagles offers leaders an opportunity for personal growth and development. By reflecting on their own

leadership styles and continuously seeking to improve, leaders can enhance their self-awareness, expand their skills, and become more effective in their roles.

In summary, emulating and learning the lessons from eagles equips leaders with valuable insights, strategies, and qualities that contribute to their personal growth, team effectiveness, and organizational success. By drawing inspiration from these majestic creatures, leaders can elevate their leadership impact and create a positive and thriving work environment.

31 Lessons
Leaders can learn from
Eagles

Vision and Focus

Eagles have exceptional eyesight, allowing them to spot prey from great distances. Leaders can learn to develop a clear vision and stay focused on their goals, like eagles focus on their prey, to achieve success.

Eagles provide a remarkable example of vision and focus. Their exceptional eyesight enables them to spot prey from great distances, showcasing their ability to maintain unwavering focus on their goal. Leaders can learn from eagles and apply their approach to develop a clear vision and stay focused on their goals. Here's a detailed explanation with examples and steps:

- ✓ Develop a Clear Vision: Like eagles, leaders should start by developing a clear vision of what they want to achieve. A vision is a compelling and inspiring picture of the desired future state. It provides a sense of direction and purpose for the leader and the team. For example, the vision of the late Steve Jobs, co-founder of Apple, was to create user-friendly technology that would revolutionize various industries.

- ✓ Define Goals and Objectives: Once the vision is established, leaders should break it down into specific goals and objectives. These goals act as milestones on the path to achieving the overall vision. For instance, if the vision is to become the market leader in a particular industry, the goals could include increasing market share, launching innovative products, or expanding into new markets.

- ✓ Communicate the Vision: Effective leaders understand the importance of communicating the vision to their team members. By sharing the vision, leaders inspire and align their team towards a common purpose. They articulate the vision in a way that resonates with their employees, helping them understand the significance of their work in the larger context. Just as eagles use their vocalizations to communicate and establish territories within their flock, leaders must use clear and concise communication to convey the vision to their teams.
- ✓ Stay Focused on Priorities: Eagles maintain a laser-like focus on their prey, ignoring distractions and staying committed to their goal. Similarly, leaders must prioritize their efforts and stay focused on the key objectives that align with the vision. They should identify the critical tasks and allocate resources accordingly. By avoiding unnecessary distractions and staying disciplined, leaders can maximize their productivity and progress towards their goals.
- ✓ Adapt and Adjust: While eagles remain focused on their prey, they also adapt their hunting strategies based on the changing circumstances. Leaders should embrace a similar approach by remaining open to feedback and adjusting their plans as needed. They should monitor progress, identify potential obstacles, and be willing to modify their strategies to ensure they are on the right track towards achieving the vision.

✓ Inspire and Motivate: Leaders can draw inspiration from eagles' focused determination and use it to inspire and motivate their teams. By sharing the vision and demonstrating unwavering commitment to its realization, leaders instill a sense of purpose and drive within their team members. They can highlight the progress made, celebrate milestones, and provide continuous feedback to keep the team motivated and aligned with the vision.

✓ Lead by Example: Just as eagles demonstrate focus by maintaining their gaze on their prey, leaders must lead by example. They should embody the vision and values they communicate, consistently demonstrating focus and commitment in their own work. When leaders showcase their dedication to the vision, it inspires their team members to follow suit.

✓ Create Accountability: Leaders should establish mechanisms to hold themselves and their team accountable for achieving the vision. This can include setting clear performance metrics, conducting regular progress reviews, and providing constructive feedback. By creating a culture of accountability, leaders ensure that everyone is working towards the vision with focus and determination.

By following these steps and emulating the focus exhibited by eagles, leaders can develop a clear vision, stay focused on their goals, and inspire their teams to achieve success. Through effective communication, adaptability, leading by example, and creating accountability, leaders can bring their vision to life and drive their organizations towards excellence.

Adaptability and Resilience

Eagles adapt to changing environments and overcome challenges. Leaders can learn to be adaptable and resilient, adjusting their strategies and overcoming obstacles to lead their teams through changing circumstances.

Eagles exemplify adaptability and resilience as they navigate changing environments and overcome challenges. Leaders can learn from eagles and apply these qualities to their own leadership approach. Here's a detailed explanation with examples and steps on how eagles exhibit adaptability and resilience, and how leaders can emulate these characteristics:

1. Embracing Changing Environments: Eagles encounter diverse environments throughout their migratory journeys. They adapt to varying climates, landscapes, and food availability. Similarly, leaders need to recognize the dynamic nature of their industries and markets. They must stay attuned to changes in customer preferences, technological advancements, and competitive landscapes. By embracing changing environments, leaders can proactively adjust strategies and remain agile in response to evolving circumstances. Example: Satya Nadella, the CEO of Microsoft, recognized the shift towards cloud computing and led the company's transformation to focus on cloud-based services. This adaptability allowed Microsoft to remain competitive and thrive in an evolving technology landscape.

Steps for Leaders to Emulate:
- ✓ Stay informed: Continuously gather market intelligence, monitor industry trends, and anticipate changes.
- ✓ Foster a learning culture: Encourage employees to stay updated on industry developments, attend training programs, and acquire new skills.
- ✓ Seek diverse perspectives: Embrace diverse viewpoints within the team to foster innovative thinking and adaptability.
- ✓ Encourage experimentation: Create an environment where trying new approaches and learning from failures is encouraged and supported.

2. Adjusting Strategies: Eagles display the ability to adjust their hunting strategies based on the availability of prey or changes in environmental conditions. Similarly, leaders must be willing to adapt their strategies when faced with new challenges or unforeseen circumstances. They should analyze the situation, gather feedback, and make necessary adjustments to keep their teams on track. Example: Jeff Bezos, the founder of Amazon, initially focused on selling books but recognized the potential for a broader e-commerce platform. He adjusted his strategy and expanded Amazon's offerings to become the global retail giant it is today.

Steps for Leaders to Emulate:
- ✓ Foster a culture of openness: Encourage employees to provide feedback and suggestions for improvement.

- ✓ Regularly evaluate strategies: Conduct periodic reviews of goals, objectives, and strategies to ensure alignment with the current landscape.
- ✓ Encourage flexibility: Empower team members to propose and implement alternative approaches when necessary.
- ✓ Monitor and measure progress: Implement performance metrics to track the effectiveness of strategies and identify areas for improvement.

3. Overcoming Challenges: Eagles face various challenges during their migratory journeys, such as harsh weather conditions and competition for resources. They exhibit resilience by persevering and adapting their hunting techniques to overcome these obstacles. Leaders must demonstrate resilience in the face of adversity, instilling confidence and determination in their teams. Example: Mary Barra, the CEO of General Motors, successfully guided the company through challenging times, including product recalls and financial difficulties. Her resilience and ability to navigate through adversity contributed to General Motors' recovery and sustained growth.

Steps for Leaders to Emulate:

- ✓ Foster a positive mindset: Encourage a culture of optimism, perseverance, and learning from failures.
- ✓ Provide support and resources: Offer guidance, resources, and training to help employees overcome challenges and build their resilience.

- ✓ Communicate with transparency: Keep employees informed about challenges, progress, and the actions being taken to address them.
- ✓ Celebrate successes: Recognize and celebrate milestones and achievements, reinforcing a sense of accomplishment and motivation.

4. Encouraging a Growth Mindset: Eagles continuously adapt and learn, incorporating new hunting techniques and adjusting to changing seasons. Leaders can foster a growth mindset within their teams, promoting continuous learning and adaptation. By encouraging employees to embrace new ideas, develop new skills, and expand their knowledge, leaders create a resilient and adaptable workforce. Example: Sundar Pichai, the CEO of Google, has emphasized the importance of a growth mindset and continuous learning. Under his leadership, Google has encouraged employees to explore new technologies and develop innovative solutions.

Steps for Leaders to Emulate:

- ✓ Create a learning culture: Encourage employees to pursue professional development opportunities, attend conferences, and participate in training programs.
- ✓ Provide resources for learning: Allocate resources for skill development, such as online courses, workshops, or mentoring programs.

- ✓ Recognize and reward learning: Acknowledge and reward employees who demonstrate a commitment to learning and personal growth.
- ✓ Lead by example: Show your own dedication to learning by sharing your own learning experiences and seeking feedback from others.

By observing how eagles adapt to changing environments and overcome challenges, leaders can cultivate their own adaptability and resilience. Emulating eagles' ability to adjust strategies, overcome obstacles, foster a growth mindset, and embrace change, leaders can guide their teams through changing circumstances and drive organizational success.

Strategic Planning

Eagles plan their hunting strategies meticulously, observing their surroundings and anticipating the movements of their prey. Leaders can apply this approach to corporate leadership by developing and implementing effective strategic plans to achieve long-term goals.

Eagles demonstrate strategic planning in their hunting behaviors, and leaders can learn from their approach to apply it to corporate leadership. Here's a detailed explanation with examples and steps on how eagles exhibit strategic planning and how leaders can emulate it:

1. Observing and Assessing: Eagles start their hunting process by observing their surroundings and assessing the movements of their prey. They carefully analyze the landscape, weather conditions, and potential prey locations. Similarly, leaders need to observe their business environment, market trends, customer behaviors, and competitor activities. By gathering relevant information, leaders can make informed decisions and develop effective strategic plans. Example: Before launching the iPhone, Apple's strategic planning involved observing consumer trends, assessing the limitations of existing smartphones, and identifying opportunities to revolutionize the mobile phone industry.

Steps for Leaders to Emulate:

✓ Conduct market research: Gather data and insights about customer needs, market dynamics, and industry trends.

- ✓ Stay informed: Keep track of changes in the competitive landscape, emerging technologies, and regulatory developments.
- ✓ Seek diverse perspectives: Engage with stakeholders, internal teams, and external experts to gain different viewpoints and identify potential opportunities and threats.
- ✓ Analyze strengths and weaknesses: Evaluate the organization's internal capabilities, resources, and core competencies to identify areas of advantage and improvement.

2. Setting Clear Goals and Objectives: Eagles have specific goals when they plan their hunting strategies - to catch prey and provide sustenance for themselves and their offspring. Leaders must establish clear goals and objectives that align with their organization's vision and mission. These goals should be specific, measurable, achievable, relevant, and time-bound (SMART). Clear goals provide direction and help align the efforts of the team. Example: Google's strategic planning involved setting clear goals to organize the world's information, make it universally accessible and useful, and create innovative products that enhance users' lives.

Steps for Leaders to Emulate:

- ✓ Define the organization's vision and mission: Craft a clear and inspiring vision statement that outlines the desired future state and a mission statement that reflects the purpose and values of the organization.
- ✓ Break down goals into objectives: Divide the goals into specific objectives that are aligned with the vision and mission. These objectives

should be actionable, measurable, and time-bound.

✓ Communicate goals and objectives: Share the goals and objectives with the team, ensuring clarity and understanding. Cascade the goals throughout the organization to align everyone's efforts.

3. Developing Strategies and Action Plans: After assessing the situation and setting goals, eagles develop strategies to achieve their hunting objectives. They formulate action plans based on their observations and anticipation of the prey's movements. Similarly, leaders should develop strategic plans that outline the actions, initiatives, and resource allocations required to accomplish the set goals. Example: Amazon's strategic planning involved developing strategies to enhance customer experience, expand product offerings, optimize supply chain operations, and drive market penetration.

Steps for Leaders to Emulate:

✓ Identify strategic initiatives: Determine the key initiatives that will drive the organization closer to its goals. These initiatives may include product development, market expansion, process optimization, or talent acquisition.

✓ Allocate resources: Assess the required resources, such as budget, personnel, and technology, to execute the strategic initiatives effectively. Allocate resources strategically based on priority and potential impact.

✓ Define key performance indicators (KPIs): Establish KPIs that will measure the success and progress of each strategic initiative. KPIs

should be aligned with the goals and objectives set in the planning phase.
✓ Develop action plans: Create detailed action plans that outline specific activities, timelines, responsibilities, and milestones for each strategic initiative.
4. Regular Evaluation and Adjustments: Eagles constantly monitor their hunting strategies and make adjustments as needed. They adapt their approaches based on the success or failure of previous attempts. Likewise, leaders should regularly evaluate the progress of their strategic plans, assess the effectiveness of implemented initiatives, and make adjustments when necessary. Example: Coca-Cola regularly evaluates its strategic plans by analyzing market trends, consumer preferences, and competitor activities. This evaluation allows the company to adjust its marketing strategies, product portfolio, and expansion plans to stay competitive.

Steps for Leaders to Emulate:
✓ Implement regular performance reviews: Set up regular evaluation cycles to review the progress of strategic initiatives and measure performance against established KPIs.
✓ Gather feedback and insights: Seek feedback from team members, customers, and stakeholders to gain insights into the effectiveness of implemented strategies. Use this feedback to identify areas for improvement.
✓ Adapt and adjust: Based on the evaluation and feedback, make necessary adjustments to the strategic plans and initiatives. This may

involve reallocating resources, changing tactics, or exploring new opportunities.

5. Communicate and Align: Effective strategic planning involves clear communication and alignment with the entire organization. Eagles communicate their hunting strategies with other eagles in their flock to ensure collaboration and coordination. Leaders should also communicate the strategic plans to their teams, ensuring understanding, commitment, and alignment towards the common objectives.

Steps for Leaders to Emulate:

✓ Develop a communication plan: Create a comprehensive communication plan that outlines how the strategic plans will be shared, the frequency of communication, and the channels to be used.

✓ Engage employees: Facilitate two-way communication to engage employees and foster a sense of ownership and commitment to the strategic plans. Encourage feedback, questions, and suggestions from team members.

✓ Cascade the plans: Ensure that the strategic plans are cascaded throughout the organization, from top-level managers to frontline employees. Provide clarity on each team member's role in executing the plans.

By observing eagles' strategic planning behaviors and implementing the corresponding steps, leaders can develop effective strategic plans that drive their organizations towards long-term success. Applying the lessons of observation and assessment, setting clear goals, developing strategies, evaluating progress, and fostering communication and alignment, leaders can navigate the complexities of their industries and guide their teams towards achieving their shared vision.

Effective Communication

Eagles use vocalizations and body language to communicate with their flock and establish territories. Leaders can learn the importance of clear and concise communication in leadership, fostering understanding and collaboration among team members.

Eagles rely on effective communication through vocalizations and body language to establish territories and communicate with their flock. Leaders can learn from eagles' communication methods and apply them to their own leadership approach. Here's a detailed explanation with examples and steps on how eagles exhibit effective communication and how leaders can emulate it:

1. Clear and Concise Communication: Eagles use specific vocalizations and body language to convey messages clearly and concisely. They have distinct calls for different purposes, such as territorial defense, courtship, or warning signals. Similarly, leaders should communicate with clarity and brevity to ensure that their messages are easily understood by team members. Example: Martin Luther King Jr., through his famous "I Have a Dream" speech, effectively communicated his vision for equality, justice, and civil rights in a concise and inspiring manner.

Steps for Leaders to Emulate:

   ✓ Prepare and organize thoughts: Before communicating, leaders should organize their thoughts and ensure they have a clear understanding of the message they want to convey.

- ✓ Choose the right medium: Select the appropriate communication medium that best suits the nature of the message and the target audience. This could include face-to-face meetings, emails, presentations, or virtual communication tools.
- ✓ Use simple and concise language: Avoid jargon or complex terminology. Instead, use clear and simple language to ensure that the message is easily understood by all recipients.
- ✓ Focus on key points: Prioritize the key points and ensure they are communicated clearly. Avoid overwhelming team members with excessive information.

2. Active Listening: Eagles engage in active listening to understand and respond to the vocalizations and body language of other eagles. They pay attention to the cues from their flock members, allowing for effective coordination and collaboration. Leaders should practice active listening to foster understanding and build strong relationships with their team members. Example: Indra Nooyi, the former CEO of PepsiCo, was known for her active listening skills. She actively engaged in listening to her employees' perspectives, ideas, and concerns, creating an inclusive and collaborative work environment.

Steps for Leaders to Emulate:

- ✓ Be fully present: Give undivided attention to the speaker, maintain eye contact, and avoid distractions.

✓ Show empathy: Demonstrate empathy by acknowledging the speaker's emotions and perspectives. This helps build trust and strengthens relationships.

✓ Ask clarifying questions: Seek clarification and further understanding by asking questions that demonstrate active engagement with the speaker's message.

✓ Provide feedback and validation: Offer feedback to the speaker to show that their thoughts and ideas have been heard and valued.

3. Non-Verbal Communication: Eagles utilize body language to communicate non-verbally, conveying information about their intentions, emotions, and dominance. They use postures, wing displays, and eye contact to establish territories and communicate within their flock. Leaders can learn from eagles by leveraging non-verbal communication to reinforce their verbal messages and create a deeper connection with their team members. Example: Nelson Mandela, through his confident and open body language, effectively communicated his authenticity and sincerity, creating a strong connection with his followers.

Steps for Leaders to Emulate:

✓ Be aware of body language: Pay attention to your own body language and its impact on others. Project confidence, openness, and approachability through positive body language cues.

✓ Use appropriate gestures: Employ gestures that enhance your verbal communication and

emphasize key points. Use facial expressions and hand movements to convey enthusiasm and engagement.
- ✓ Maintain eye contact: Maintain appropriate eye contact during conversations to demonstrate attentiveness and interest.
- ✓ Adapt to cultural differences: Be mindful of cultural norms and adapt your non-verbal communication style accordingly, ensuring inclusivity and respect.
4. Two-Way Communication: Eagles engage in two-way communication within their flock, responding to the vocalizations and body language of other eagles. They create a dialogue that enables collaboration and coordination. Similarly, leaders should encourage open and two-way communication, providing opportunities for team members to share their thoughts, ideas, and concerns. Example: Elon Musk, CEO of Tesla and SpaceX, uses various communication channels, such as company-wide emails and internal Q&A sessions, to facilitate open communication and create a dialogue within his organizations.

Steps for Leaders to Emulate:
- ✓ Create a safe environment: Foster a safe and inclusive environment where team members feel comfortable expressing their opinions and ideas.
- ✓ Encourage feedback: Regularly seek feedback from team members and demonstrate openness to their suggestions and concerns.

- ✓ Practice active feedback: Provide constructive feedback to team members, recognizing their achievements and offering guidance for improvement.
- ✓ Establish regular communication channels: Implement regular team meetings, one-on-one discussions, and open forums to facilitate ongoing communication.

5. Tailor Communication to the Audience: Eagles adjust their vocalizations and body language based on their audience and purpose. They adapt their communication to convey specific messages to different individuals within their flock. Similarly, leaders should tailor their communication to the audience, considering their preferences, knowledge, and cultural backgrounds. Example: Angela Merkel, the former Chancellor of Germany, was known for her ability to adapt her communication style to connect with diverse audiences, whether it was addressing political leaders or engaging with citizens.

Steps for Leaders to Emulate:
- ✓ Understand the audience: Gain insights into the backgrounds, perspectives, and communication preferences of team members.
- ✓ Use appropriate language and tone: Adapt your language and tone to resonate with the audience. Avoid jargon and technical terms that may be unfamiliar to them.
- ✓ Customize the message: Craft the message in a way that is relevant and relatable to the specific audience, highlighting how it aligns with their interests and goals.

✓ Seek feedback: Ask for feedback on your communication style and effectiveness to continuously improve and refine your approach.

By observing how eagles communicate through vocalizations and body language and applying the corresponding steps, leaders can enhance their own communication skills. By adopting clear and concise communication, active listening, non-verbal cues, two-way communication, and audience adaptation, leaders can foster understanding, collaboration, and engagement among their team members, leading to stronger relationships and more effective communication within the organization.

Leading by Example

Eagles lead from the front, soaring high and displaying their majestic flight. Leaders can learn to lead by example, demonstrating the behaviors and values they expect from their team members, and inspiring them through their actions.

Eagles exhibit leading by example through their majestic flight and dominant presence. Leaders can learn from eagles' approach and apply it to their own leadership style. Here's a detailed explanation with examples and steps on how eagles exhibit leading by example and how leaders can emulate it:

1. Demonstrating Behaviors and Values: Eagles lead from the front by demonstrating the behaviors and values they expect from their fellow eagles. They showcase their majestic flight, grace, and dominance, setting an example for others to follow. Similarly, leaders must embody the behaviors and values they wish to see in their team members. Example: Mahatma Gandhi exemplified leading by example through his nonviolent resistance and commitment to peace. His actions inspired millions and led to significant social and political changes in India.

Steps for Leaders to Emulate:

- ✓ Define desired behaviors and values: Clearly define the behaviors and values that align with the organization's vision and mission.
- ✓ Live by the values: Consistently display and practice these behaviors and values in your own actions and decisions.

- ✓ Be authentic: Lead with authenticity and integrity, ensuring that your words align with your actions.
- ✓ Set high standards: Hold yourself to high standards and strive for excellence in all aspects of your work.
2. Inspiring Through Actions: Eagles inspire and captivate others through their majestic flight. Their soaring and dominant presence evokes a sense of awe and admiration. Leaders can inspire their team members by consistently demonstrating excellence and achieving remarkable results. Example: Richard Branson, the founder of Virgin Group, inspires his employees through his adventurous and entrepreneurial spirit. His enthusiasm and determination in pursuing bold ventures have motivated his team members to embrace innovation and take risks.

Steps for Leaders to Emulate:
- ✓ Set challenging goals: Establish ambitious goals that stretch the capabilities of your team members and inspire them to push their limits.
- ✓ Take calculated risks: Demonstrate a willingness to take calculated risks and encourage your team to do the same, fostering a culture of innovation and learning.
- ✓ Celebrate achievements: Recognize and celebrate the achievements of your team members, reinforcing their efforts and inspiring them to strive for excellence.
- ✓ Share success stories: Share success stories and personal experiences to inspire and motivate your team. Showcasing real-life examples of overcoming challenges and

achieving success can ignite their passion and drive.

3. Providing Guidance and Support: Eagles provide guidance and support to their fellow eagles, particularly to the young ones learning to fly. They stay close, offering encouragement and helping them gain confidence. Similarly, leaders should provide guidance and support to their team members, helping them develop their skills and grow. Example: Mary Barra, the CEO of General Motors, actively engages with her employees and provides support and guidance. Her accessible leadership style and willingness to listen have created a supportive and empowering work environment.

Steps for Leaders to Emulate:

- ✓ Mentorship and coaching: Provide mentorship and coaching to team members, guiding them in their professional development and helping them overcome challenges.
- ✓ Encourage growth and learning: Support and facilitate opportunities for continuous learning and growth, both through formal training programs and on-the-job experiences.
- ✓ Offer constructive feedback: Provide timely and constructive feedback to help team members improve their performance and develop their skills.
- ✓ Create a supportive environment: Foster a culture of support and collaboration, where team members feel comfortable seeking help and learning from each other.

4. Encouraging Collaboration and Teamwork: Eagles work together in their flock,

coordinating their efforts for hunting and raising their young ones. Leaders can foster collaboration and teamwork by actively encouraging cooperation and creating an environment that values collective success. Example: Sundar Pichai, the CEO of Google, promotes a culture of collaboration and teamwork within the organization. He encourages cross-functional collaboration, knowledge sharing, and the exchange of ideas among employees.

Steps for Leaders to Emulate:

- ✓ Establish shared goals: Create a sense of collective purpose by defining shared goals that require collaboration and cooperation.
- ✓ Facilitate communication: Encourage open communication and information sharing among team members, promoting a collaborative work environment.
- ✓ Build diverse teams: Foster diverse and inclusive teams that bring together individuals with different perspectives, experiences, and skills.
- ✓ Recognize and reward teamwork: Acknowledge and reward collaborative efforts, celebrating team achievements and emphasizing the importance of teamwork.

5. Empowering Others: Eagles empower their flock members by allowing them to take on responsibilities and learn from their experiences. Leaders can empower their team members by delegating authority, providing autonomy, and trusting them to make decisions. Example: Anne Mulcahy, the former CEO of Xerox, successfully turned around the

company by empowering her employees. She decentralized decision-making, giving employees the freedom to innovate and contribute to the company's success.

Steps for Leaders to Emulate:
- ✓ Delegate authority: Assign tasks and projects that allow team members to take ownership and make decisions.
- ✓ Provide autonomy: Grant autonomy to team members, allowing them to explore their creativity, problem-solving skills, and decision-making abilities.
- ✓ Trust and support: Trust your team members to deliver results and provide the necessary support and resources to ensure their success.
- ✓ Encourage initiative: Foster an environment where individuals are encouraged to take initiative, share ideas, and contribute to the organization's growth.

By observing how eagles lead from the front and applying the corresponding steps, leaders can effectively lead by example. By demonstrating desired behaviors and values, inspiring through actions, providing guidance and support, encouraging collaboration and teamwork, and empowering others, leaders can inspire and motivate their team members to achieve their full potential and drive organizational success.

Coaching, Guidance and Support

Eagles provide an excellent example of coaching in the animal kingdom. When eagles are teaching their young ones to fly, they exhibit behaviors that parallel effective coaching practices in management. Here's how eagles coach their young ones to fly and the lessons it offers for coaching in management:

- ✓ Demonstrating the Process: Eagles start by demonstrating the flying process themselves. The adult eagle takes flight, showcasing the techniques and maneuvers required for successful flight. This demonstration sets a clear example for the young eagles to follow. Similarly, effective coaching in management involves demonstrating the desired skills, behaviors, and strategies to employees. Managers can lead by example, showcasing the correct approach and providing a visual reference for their team members.
- ✓ Providing Guidance and Support: As the young eagles begin their attempts at flying, the adult eagles provide guidance and support. They stay close to their young ones, offering encouragement and helping them gain confidence. In management coaching, it is crucial to provide guidance and support to employees. Managers should offer constructive feedback, provide resources and tools, and be available for guidance, creating a supportive environment that fosters learning and growth.
- ✓ Gradual Release of Control: As the young eagles gain more confidence and skill, the

adult eagles gradually release control and give them more independence. They allow the young eagles to flap their wings and experience the sensation of flight, while still monitoring their progress closely. Similarly, effective coaching in management involves gradually giving employees more autonomy and responsibility as they develop their skills and capabilities. Managers can delegate tasks and provide opportunities for employees to take ownership, allowing them to grow and learn from their experiences.

- ✓ Correcting Mistakes: Eagles understand that mistakes are part of the learning process. When the young eagles make mistakes while attempting to fly, the adult eagles correct them gently but firmly. They provide guidance on how to adjust their wings, maintain balance, and improve their technique. In management coaching, it is essential to recognize that mistakes are valuable learning opportunities. Managers should provide constructive feedback, correct mistakes without discouraging employees, and guide them toward improvement.

- ✓ Celebrating Success: When the young eagles successfully take flight, the adult eagles celebrate their accomplishment. They provide positive reinforcement and encouragement, acknowledging the progress made by the young ones. In management coaching, celebrating success is equally important. Managers should recognize and celebrate the achievements and milestones of their employees, fostering a positive and motivating work environment.

Lessons for Coaching in Management: Eagles' coaching behavior provides valuable lessons for coaching in management:

- ✓ Lead by Example: Managers should lead by example, demonstrating the desired skills and behaviors they want to see in their team members.
- ✓ Provide Guidance and Support: Managers should offer guidance and support to employees, helping them develop their skills and gain confidence.
- ✓ Gradually Delegate Responsibility: Managers should gradually release control and delegate tasks, allowing employees to grow and take ownership of their work.
- ✓ Provide Constructive Feedback: Managers should provide constructive feedback, correcting mistakes and guiding employees toward improvement.
- ✓ Celebrate Success: Managers should celebrate the achievements and successes of their employees, fostering a positive and motivating work environment.

By applying these lessons from eagles' coaching behavior, managers can effectively coach their team members, nurture their growth, and help them reach their full potential in the workplace.

Teamwork and Collaboration

Eagles work cooperatively within their social structure, sharing responsibilities and protecting their territory. Leaders can learn the importance of teamwork and collaboration, fostering a collaborative environment that harnesses the collective intelligence and skills of their team members.

Eagles exhibit teamwork and collaboration within their social structure, working cooperatively to share responsibilities and protect their territory. Leaders can learn from eagles' collaborative behaviors and apply them to foster teamwork and collaboration within their teams. Here's a detailed explanation with examples and steps on how eagles exhibit teamwork and collaboration and how leaders can emulate it:

1. Cooperative Behavior: Eagles engage in cooperative behavior within their flock, coordinating their efforts for hunting, nesting, and territorial defense. They work together to achieve common goals and protect their shared interests. Similarly, leaders should foster a sense of cooperation and collaboration among team members. Example: The Apollo 11 mission that successfully landed humans on the moon demonstrated exceptional teamwork and collaboration among NASA engineers, astronauts, and ground control. Each individual played a crucial role, contributing their expertise to the mission's success.

Steps for Leaders to Emulate:
- ✓ Establish a shared purpose: Clearly communicate the team's common goals and

purpose, creating a sense of shared mission and ownership.

✓ Encourage mutual support: Promote a culture of mutual support, where team members willingly help and assist one another to achieve collective objectives.

✓ Foster a sense of unity: Emphasize the importance of teamwork and collaboration, highlighting how individual contributions contribute to the greater success of the team.

✓ Recognize and celebrate collaboration: Acknowledge and reward instances of effective collaboration, reinforcing its value and encouraging further collaboration within the team.

2. Open Communication: Eagles engage in vocalizations and body language to communicate with their flock members. They share information, coordinate hunting strategies, and signal danger or territorial boundaries. Effective communication is crucial for successful teamwork and collaboration. Leaders should promote open communication within their teams. Example: Pixar Animation Studios, known for its highly collaborative creative process, encourages open communication among team members. Regular feedback sessions and brainstorming meetings create an environment where ideas can be freely shared and improved upon.

Steps for Leaders to Emulate:

✓ Foster a safe environment: Create a psychologically safe space where team members feel comfortable expressing their

thoughts, ideas, and concerns without fear of judgment or reprisal.
- ✓ Encourage active listening: Encourage team members to actively listen to one another, fostering mutual understanding and respect.
- ✓ Establish regular communication channels: Implement regular team meetings, virtual collaboration platforms, or other communication tools to facilitate ongoing communication and information sharing.
- ✓ Provide constructive feedback: Encourage team members to provide constructive feedback to one another, promoting growth and improvement within the team.

3. Leveraging Diverse Perspectives: Eagles in a flock come from diverse backgrounds, each bringing their unique strengths and skills. They leverage these diverse perspectives to tackle challenges and enhance their collective intelligence. Similarly, leaders should value and leverage the diversity of their team members to foster innovation and collaboration. Example: Procter & Gamble (P&G) encourages diverse collaboration through their Connect+Develop program. P&G collaborates with external partners and diverse thinkers to drive innovation and develop new products.

Steps for Leaders to Emulate:
- ✓ Create a diverse team: Assemble a team with diverse backgrounds, experiences, and skill sets, ensuring representation from different perspectives.

- ✓ Foster inclusion and respect: Create an inclusive environment where diverse viewpoints are respected and valued.
- ✓ Encourage active participation: Encourage team members to actively contribute their ideas and perspectives, ensuring that everyone's voice is heard.
- ✓ Facilitate collaboration across teams: Break down silos and promote cross-functional collaboration to leverage diverse expertise and drive innovation.

4. Establishing Clear Roles and Responsibilities: Within an eagle's social structure, each member has specific roles and responsibilities. From nest-building to hunting, they divide tasks to optimize efficiency. Leaders should define clear roles and responsibilities within their teams to ensure smooth collaboration and minimize confusion. Example: In a surgical team, each member has a specific role, such as surgeon, anesthesiologist, and nurses. Clear roles and responsibilities enable efficient teamwork during surgeries.

Steps for Leaders to Emulate:

- ✓ Clearly define roles and responsibilities: Clearly communicate the specific roles and responsibilities of each team member, ensuring everyone understands their contributions and expectations.
- ✓ Foster cross-training: Encourage team members to acquire knowledge and skills beyond their primary roles, facilitating flexibility and supporting one another when needed.

✓ Promote interdependence: Emphasize the importance of interdependence, highlighting how each team member's contributions are vital for the overall success of the team.
✓ Regularly reassess roles and responsibilities: As the team evolves or project requirements change, periodically review and adjust roles and responsibilities to optimize efficiency and adapt to new circumstances.

5. Promoting Trust and Psychological Safety: Eagles within a flock trust and rely on one another for their collective well-being and protection. Leaders should promote trust and psychological safety within their teams, fostering an environment where individuals feel comfortable taking risks, sharing ideas, and collaborating. Example: Google's Project Aristotle research identified psychological safety as a key factor for effective teamwork. Teams that fostered trust and psychological safety were more likely to experiment, share knowledge, and perform at a high level.

Steps for Leaders to Emulate:
✓ Lead with trust: Trust your team members and demonstrate trustworthiness through your actions and decisions.
✓ Encourage risk-taking and learning from failure: Create an environment where team members feel comfortable taking calculated risks and learning from their mistakes without fear of retribution.
✓ Foster open dialogue: Encourage team members to openly share their ideas, opinions, and concerns, creating an atmosphere of psychological safety.

- ✓ Support collaboration through shared goals: Align individual goals with collective goals to promote collaboration and cooperation rather than unhealthy competition.

By observing how eagles exhibit teamwork and collaboration and applying the corresponding steps, leaders can foster a collaborative environment that harnesses the collective intelligence and skills of their team members. By promoting cooperative behavior, open communication, leveraging diverse perspectives, establishing clear roles and responsibilities, and fostering trust and psychological safety, leaders can drive effective teamwork and collaboration, leading to enhanced performance and achievement of shared goals.

Decision-Making and Risk Assessment

Eagles make calculated decisions in their hunting and nesting activities, evaluating risks and opportunities. Leaders can learn to make informed decisions and assess risks effectively, guiding their organizations through uncertainty and making sound choices.

Eagles exhibit decision-making and risk assessment skills in their hunting and nesting activities. Leaders can learn from eagles' approach and apply it to their own decision-making processes. Here's a detailed explanation with examples and steps on how eagles exhibit decision-making and risk assessment, and how leaders can emulate it:

1. Calculated Decision-Making: Eagles make calculated decisions when it comes to hunting and nesting. They evaluate various factors, such as prey behavior, weather conditions, and their own capabilities, before initiating an attack or selecting a nesting site. Similarly, leaders should make informed decisions by considering relevant factors and assessing potential outcomes. Example: Amazon's decision to enter the cloud computing market with Amazon Web Services (AWS) was a calculated decision made by Jeff Bezos and his team. They assessed the market potential, identified the gaps, and strategically positioned AWS as a leading cloud services provider.

Steps for Leaders to Emulate:

- ✓ Gather relevant information: Seek and gather accurate and up-to-date information related to the decision at hand. This may involve market research, data analysis, expert opinions, or internal reports.
- ✓ Analyze pros and cons: Evaluate the potential benefits and drawbacks of each option. Consider factors such as financial implications, market demand, competitive landscape, and alignment with organizational goals.
- ✓ Consult stakeholders: Involve relevant stakeholders in the decision-making process. Seek input and perspectives from individuals who may be impacted by the decision or possess valuable insights.
- ✓ Evaluate long-term consequences: Consider the potential long-term consequences of the decision, including its impact on the organization's vision, mission, and values.

2. Risk Assessment: Eagles assess risks before engaging in hunting or nesting activities. They evaluate the likelihood of success, potential dangers, and the availability of resources. Leaders should also assess risks in their decision-making processes to mitigate potential negative consequences. Example: SpaceX, led by Elon Musk, assesses the risks associated with each rocket launch. They evaluate factors such as weather conditions, technical challenges, and potential malfunctions to ensure safe and successful missions.

Steps for Leaders to Emulate:

✓ Identify potential risks: Identify and list the potential risks associated with each decision or course of action. Consider internal and external factors that could impact the outcome.

✓ Evaluate likelihood and impact: Assess the likelihood of each risk occurring and the potential impact it may have on the organization. Prioritize risks based on their severity and likelihood.

✓ Develop risk mitigation strategies: Develop strategies to mitigate or minimize identified risks. This may involve contingency plans, risk-sharing arrangements, or implementing safety measures.

✓ Seek expert advice: Consult subject-matter experts or individuals with expertise in the specific area of risk to gain insights and guidance.

3. Scenario Planning: Eagles engage in mental scenario planning before initiating a hunting dive or selecting a nesting site. They anticipate potential obstacles, predict the prey's movements, and envision different outcomes. Leaders can use scenario planning techniques to assess potential scenarios and make more informed decisions. Example: Shell, the multinational energy company, utilizes scenario planning to assess potential future scenarios in the energy market. This allows them to make strategic decisions that are resilient to different market conditions.

Steps for Leaders to Emulate:

✓ Identify key uncertainties: Identify the key uncertainties or factors that may significantly impact the decision. These uncertainties could include changes in technology, market dynamics, regulatory environment, or customer behavior.

✓ Develop alternative scenarios: Create different scenarios based on the identified uncertainties. Each scenario should present a different set of circumstances or outcomes.

✓ Assess implications for each scenario: Evaluate the implications of each scenario on the decision or course of action. Consider the risks, opportunities, and resource requirements associated with each scenario.

✓ Determine robust strategies: Develop strategies that are robust and adaptable across multiple scenarios. Consider strategies that can withstand different market conditions or uncertain environments.

4. Embracing a Test-and-Learn Approach: Eagles learn through trial and error in their hunting endeavors. They adapt their strategies and techniques based on the outcome of their attempts. Leaders can embrace a test-and-learn approach, where decisions are made based on experimentation and iterative learning. Example: Google's approach to product development involves releasing beta versions and gathering user feedback to make iterative improvements. This test-and-learn approach enables them to refine their products and services based on user preferences and needs.

Steps for Leaders to Emulate:

✓ Encourage experimentation: Create an environment that encourages experimentation and learning from failures. Emphasize the value of lessons learned from unsuccessful attempts.

✓ Set up feedback loops: Establish feedback mechanisms to gather insights and feedback from customers, employees, or other stakeholders. Use this feedback to refine decisions and improve future outcomes.

✓ Iterate and adapt: Continuously iterate and adapt decisions based on feedback and insights gained. Embrace a flexible mindset and be willing to adjust plans or strategies as new information emerges.

✓ Foster a learning culture: Foster a culture of continuous learning and improvement within the organization. Encourage employees to share their learnings and promote knowledge-sharing initiatives.

By observing how eagles exhibit decision-making and risk assessment and applying the corresponding steps, leaders can make informed decisions and navigate uncertainties effectively. By making calculated decisions, assessing risks, engaging in scenario planning, and embracing a test-and-learn approach, leaders can enhance their decision-making abilities and guide their organizations towards success.

Continuous Learning and Growth

Eagles continually adapt and learn, incorporating new hunting techniques and adapting to changing seasons. Leaders can learn the importance of continuous learning and personal growth, embracing new knowledge and skills to stay relevant in a rapidly changing world.

Eagles exhibit continuous learning and growth through their ability to adapt, learn new hunting techniques, and adjust to changing seasons. Leaders can learn from eagles' approach and apply it to their own leadership journey. Here's a detailed explanation with examples and steps on how eagles exhibit continuous learning and growth and how leaders can emulate it:

1. Adaptation to Changing Environments: Eagles adapt to changing environments and seasons. They modify their hunting techniques, adjust flight patterns, and even migrate to different regions to find suitable conditions for survival. Similarly, leaders need to adapt and learn in response to changing market dynamics, technological advancements, and evolving customer needs. Example: Apple's late co-founder, Steve Jobs, recognized the need for continuous innovation and adaptation in the technology industry. Under his leadership, Apple consistently introduced groundbreaking products, such as the iPod, iPhone, and iPad, to stay ahead of the competition and meet evolving customer demands.

Steps for Leaders to Emulate:

✓ Stay informed about industry trends: Keep a pulse on industry trends, market shifts, and emerging technologies through continuous learning and staying up-to-date with relevant industry publications, conferences, and networking events.
✓ Embrace a growth mindset: Cultivate a mindset that embraces learning, improvement, and the willingness to adapt. Encourage team members to adopt a growth mindset as well.
✓ Foster a learning culture: Create a culture that values continuous learning and growth. Encourage employees to engage in professional development, provide opportunities for training and learning, and support initiatives that promote knowledge sharing within the organization.
✓ Seek diverse perspectives: Engage with diverse individuals, such as industry experts, thought leaders, or mentors, who can provide fresh insights and different perspectives.

2. Pursuing New Knowledge and Skills: Eagles continuously acquire new knowledge and skills to enhance their hunting capabilities. They learn from their experiences, observe other eagles, and adapt their techniques accordingly. Similarly, leaders should actively seek new knowledge and skills to improve their leadership abilities and keep pace with industry changes. Example: Satya Nadella, the CEO of Microsoft, emphasized the importance of continuous learning and personal growth. Under his leadership, Microsoft shifted its focus towards cloud computing and AI technologies, reflecting his

commitment to staying relevant in a rapidly evolving tech landscape.

Steps for Leaders to Emulate:

- ✓ Identify areas for development: Reflect on your strengths and areas for improvement as a leader. Identify specific knowledge or skills that would benefit both you and your organization.
- ✓ Set learning goals: Establish clear learning goals and create a plan to acquire new knowledge and skills. This could involve attending training programs, pursuing certifications, or engaging in self-directed learning through books, online courses, or podcasts.
- ✓ Foster a learning environment: Encourage a learning culture within your team or organization. Provide resources and support for employee development, such as access to learning platforms, mentorship programs, or cross-functional projects.
- ✓ Lead by example: Demonstrate your commitment to continuous learning by sharing your own learning journey and engaging in ongoing professional development. Encourage your team members to do the same.

3. Learning from Failure and Feedback: Eagles learn from both successful hunting attempts and failed ones. They adapt their strategies based on the outcomes and learn from experience. Similarly, leaders should embrace failure as a learning opportunity and actively seek feedback to improve their leadership skills. Example: Elon Musk, the CEO of

SpaceX and Tesla, is known for his willingness to take risks and learn from failures. He acknowledges failures as stepping stones to success and actively seeks feedback to iterate and improve his ventures.

Steps for Leaders to Emulate:

- ✓ Embrace a growth mindset: Adopt a mindset that sees failures as learning opportunities and fosters resilience. Encourage your team members to view failure in the same light.
- ✓ Foster a feedback culture: Create an environment where feedback is encouraged and valued. Provide regular opportunities for constructive feedback from team members, peers, and mentors.
- ✓ Reflect on experiences: Take time to reflect on your experiences, both successes, and failures. Extract lessons learned and identify areas for improvement.
- ✓ Apply learnings to future endeavors: Apply the insights gained from failures and feedback to enhance decision-making, problem-solving, and overall leadership effectiveness.

4. Encouraging Knowledge Sharing: Eagles observe and learn from other eagles within their flock. They share hunting techniques and knowledge, collectively enhancing their hunting abilities. Leaders should foster a culture of knowledge sharing within their teams, enabling collective growth and learning. Example: Atlassian, an Australian software company, encourages knowledge sharing through their internal platform called Confluence. Employees are encouraged to document and share their knowledge,

experiences, and best practices, creating a culture of continuous learning and collaboration.

Steps for Leaders to Emulate:
- ✓ Provide platforms for knowledge sharing: Implement collaborative tools or platforms where team members can share their expertise, best practices, and lessons learned.
- ✓ Recognize and reward knowledge sharing: Acknowledge and celebrate individuals who actively contribute to knowledge sharing initiatives. Recognize the value of knowledge exchange within the team or organization.
- ✓ Encourage mentoring and coaching: Promote mentoring and coaching relationships within the team, where experienced team members share their knowledge and insights with others.
- ✓ Facilitate cross-functional collaboration: Encourage collaboration across different teams or departments, enabling the exchange of ideas, perspectives, and expertise.

By observing how eagles exhibit continuous learning and growth and applying the corresponding steps, leaders can cultivate a learning mindset and embrace ongoing personal and professional development. By adapting to changing environments, pursuing new knowledge and skills, learning from failure and feedback, and fostering knowledge sharing, leaders can continuously improve their leadership abilities and guide their organizations towards success in a rapidly changing world.

Inspiring and Motivating Others

Eagles inspire and motivate their flock through their behavior, soaring to great heights and nurturing their young. Leaders can learn to inspire and motivate their teams by communicating a compelling vision, leading by example, and providing meaningful feedback and recognition.

Eagles exhibit inspiring and motivating behaviors within their flock through their soaring flights and nurturing of their young. Leaders can learn from eagles' approach and apply it to inspire and motivate their teams. Here's a detailed explanation with examples and steps on how eagles exhibit inspiring and motivating behaviors and how leaders can emulate them:

1. Communicating a Compelling Vision: Eagles inspire their flock by communicating a clear vision through their behavior and flight patterns. They lead the way, demonstrating their purpose and direction. Similarly, leaders should communicate a compelling vision that inspires and aligns their team members. Example: Martin Luther King Jr.'s "I Have a Dream" speech inspired millions, rallying people around a vision of equality and justice. His powerful words and unwavering conviction galvanized a movement and created lasting change.

Steps for Leaders to Emulate:
- ✓ Develop a clear vision: Define a compelling vision for your team or organization that captures the desired future state and

resonates with the aspirations of your team members.

- ✓ Communicate the vision effectively: Articulate the vision in a clear, concise, and inspiring manner. Use storytelling techniques to create an emotional connection and engage your team members.
- ✓ Align goals with the vision: Ensure that individual and team goals are aligned with the overarching vision. Help team members understand how their contributions contribute to the realization of the vision.
- ✓ Reinforce the vision: Consistently reinforce the vision through regular communication, reminders, and by tying it to day-to-day activities and decisions.

2. Leading by Example: Eagles inspire and motivate their flock through their own actions and behaviors. They lead from the front, soaring to great heights and displaying their majestic flight. Leaders can inspire their teams by leading by example and demonstrating the behaviors and values they expect from their team members. Example: Nelson Mandela, the former President of South Africa, inspired his nation through his unwavering commitment to equality, forgiveness, and reconciliation. His personal sacrifices and steadfast leadership served as a powerful example for others to follow.

Steps for Leaders to Emulate:

- ✓ Demonstrate desired behaviors: Consistently exhibit the behaviors and values you expect from your team members. Act with integrity, empathy, and resilience.

- ✓ Be accessible and approachable: Foster an open-door policy and be approachable to team members. Encourage open communication and create an environment where individuals feel comfortable sharing ideas and concerns.
- ✓ Take calculated risks: Show a willingness to take calculated risks and pursue bold initiatives. Encourage your team members to step out of their comfort zones and embrace innovation.
- ✓ Celebrate team achievements: Recognize and celebrate team achievements, both big and small. Acknowledge the efforts and contributions of individuals and teams to foster a sense of pride and motivation.
3. Providing Meaningful Feedback and Recognition: Eagles provide nurturing and guidance to their young, offering encouragement and feedback as they develop their flying skills. Leaders can motivate their teams by providing meaningful feedback and recognition for their contributions. Example: Indra Nooyi, the former CEO of PepsiCo, actively sought to empower and recognize her employees. She initiated the "Performance with Purpose" program, which recognized and rewarded employees who contributed to the company's sustainable growth.

Steps for Leaders to Emulate:

- ✓ Regularly provide feedback: Offer constructive feedback to individuals and teams to help them improve their performance and enhance their skills. Make feedback specific, actionable, and timely.

- ✓ Recognize achievements: Celebrate individual and team achievements through verbal recognition, rewards, or incentives. Highlight the impact of their contributions on the organization's success.
- ✓ Encourage peer recognition: Foster a culture of peer recognition, where team members can appreciate and acknowledge each other's efforts. Encourage team members to provide recognition and support to one another.
- ✓ Personalize recognition: Tailor recognition and rewards to individual preferences and motivations. Understand what motivates each team member and provide recognition in a way that resonates with them.

4. Fostering a Positive and Supportive Environment: Eagles create a positive and supportive environment within their flock, nurturing their young and providing protection. Leaders can create a similar environment by fostering positivity, trust, and support among team members. Example: Mary Barra, the CEO of General Motors, focuses on creating a positive and inclusive work environment. She has implemented initiatives to promote diversity, equity, and inclusion within the organization, which fosters a sense of belonging and motivation among employees.

Steps for Leaders to Emulate:
- ✓ Encourage collaboration and teamwork: Create opportunities for collaboration and foster a sense of camaraderie among team members. Promote teamwork and discourage excessive competition.

✓ Support individual growth and development: Provide resources, training, and opportunities for professional growth and development. Encourage team members to set personal goals and support them in achieving those goals.
✓ Foster open communication: Create an environment where open and transparent communication is encouraged. Value and listen to diverse perspectives and encourage constructive dialogue.
✓ Lead with empathy: Show empathy and understanding towards the needs and challenges of team members. Support their work-life balance and create policies that prioritize employee well-being.

By observing how eagles inspire and motivate their flock and applying the corresponding steps, leaders can inspire and motivate their teams to reach their full potential. By communicating a compelling vision, leading by example, providing meaningful feedback and recognition, and fostering a positive and supportive environment, leaders can create a motivated and engaged team that drives organizational success.

Embracing Change

Eagles migrate to find favorable environments, adapting to changing seasons. Leaders can learn to embrace change, adapt to new circumstances, and guide their organizations through transitions, ensuring success in dynamic environments.

Eagles exhibit a remarkable ability to embrace change by migrating to find favorable environments and adapting to changing seasons. Leaders can learn from eagles' approach and apply it to navigate and embrace change within their organizations. Here's a detailed explanation with examples and steps on how eagles exhibit embracing change and how leaders can emulate it:

1. Embracing Adaptability: Eagles showcase adaptability by migrating to different regions in search of favorable conditions. They adjust their behaviors, hunting strategies, and even their physical appearance to suit the changing environment. Similarly, leaders should embrace adaptability to effectively respond to changing circumstances and guide their organizations through transitions. Example: Netflix, initially a DVD-by-mail rental service, embraced the shift to digital streaming, adapting their business model to become a leading streaming platform. Their ability to adapt to the changing preferences of consumers ensured their continued success.

Steps for Leaders to Emulate:

✓ Foster a growth mindset: Cultivate a mindset that sees change as an opportunity for growth and improvement. Encourage your team members to embrace change and view it as a chance to learn and innovate.

- ✓ Stay informed and anticipate change: Continuously monitor the external environment and industry trends to anticipate potential changes. Stay up-to-date with technological advancements, market shifts, and customer preferences.
- ✓ Encourage experimentation and risk-taking: Create an environment where calculated risks and experimentation are encouraged. Encourage your team members to explore new ideas, pilot projects, and learn from failures.
- ✓ Provide resources and support: Ensure that your team has the necessary resources, tools, and training to adapt to changing circumstances. Support them in acquiring new skills or knowledge that may be required to navigate the change successfully.

2. Agility in Decision-Making: Eagles demonstrate agility in decision-making as they adjust their flight paths and hunting strategies based on changing environmental conditions. They quickly assess and respond to new information. Leaders should exhibit agility in decision-making to respond promptly and effectively to change. Example: Amazon's CEO, Jeff Bezos, has been known for his ability to make quick decisions in response to changing market dynamics. This agility has enabled Amazon to expand into various industries and stay at the forefront of e-commerce innovation.

Steps for Leaders to Emulate:

- ✓ Develop decision-making frameworks: Establish decision-making frameworks or guidelines that allow for swift but informed decisions. These frameworks should consider the impact of the decision, the urgency of the situation, and the level of risk involved.
- ✓ Encourage decentralized decision-making: Empower your team members to make decisions within their areas of expertise. Create an environment where decisions can be made closer to the point of action, enabling faster responses to change.
- ✓ Foster a culture of learning from failures: Encourage a culture where mistakes and failures are seen as opportunities for learning and growth. Celebrate both successful outcomes and lessons learned from failures.
- ✓ Continuously evaluate and adjust: Regularly evaluate the effectiveness of decisions and adjust strategies as new information becomes available. Remain open to feedback and be willing to pivot if necessary.
3. Effective Communication and Change Management: Eagles exhibit effective communication during their migratory patterns, maintaining coordination and sharing information within their flock. Leaders should effectively communicate and manage change within their organizations to ensure understanding, alignment, and successful implementation. Example: Microsoft's CEO, Satya Nadella, implemented a significant cultural change within the company, shifting the focus from a "know-it-all" culture to a "learn-it-all" culture. He effectively

communicated the need for change and fostered a growth mindset among employees.

Steps for Leaders to Emulate:

- ✓ Clearly communicate the need for change: Articulate the reasons and benefits behind the change to create a sense of urgency and buy-in among team members. Clearly explain how the change aligns with the organization's goals and vision.
- ✓ Provide a compelling vision of the future: Paint a vivid picture of the desired future state that the change aims to achieve. Connect the change to the organization's purpose and values to inspire and motivate team members.
- ✓ Engage in two-way communication: Encourage open and transparent communication throughout the change process. Listen to concerns, address questions, and provide regular updates to keep team members informed and engaged.
- ✓ Involve and empower employees: Involve employees in the change process by seeking their input and ideas. Empower them to take ownership of the change and contribute to its success.
- ✓ Provide support and resources: Ensure that team members have the necessary support, resources, and training to navigate the change successfully. Offer coaching, training programs, or external resources if needed.

4. Foster Resilience and Adaptation: Eagles exhibit resilience and adaptability as they endure long migrations, harsh weather conditions, and changing habitats. They persevere through challenges and adapt their

behaviors as necessary. Leaders should foster resilience and adaptation within their teams to navigate change effectively. Example: The resilience displayed by Airbnb during the COVID-19 pandemic is notable. As travel restrictions and lockdowns disrupted the industry, Airbnb quickly adapted its business model, introducing online experiences and long-term rentals to meet the changing needs of travelers.

Steps for Leaders to Emulate:

- ✓ Foster a resilient mindset: Cultivate a culture that embraces resilience and perseverance in the face of challenges. Encourage team members to view setbacks as opportunities for growth and learning.

- ✓ Encourage learning from adversity: Promote a culture of learning from failure and setbacks. Encourage individuals and teams to reflect on their experiences, extract lessons learned, and apply those insights to future endeavors.

- ✓ Provide support and resources: Offer support, resources, and training to help team members build their resilience and adaptability. This can include resilience workshops, stress management resources, or professional development opportunities.

- ✓ Celebrate adaptability and success: Recognize and celebrate instances where team members successfully adapt to change or overcome challenges. Highlight their ability to embrace change and inspire others to do the same.

By observing how eagles embrace change and applying the corresponding steps, leaders can effectively guide their organizations through transitions and ensure success in dynamic environments. By embracing adaptability, exhibiting agility in decision-making, practicing effective communication and change management, fostering resilience and adaptation, leaders can navigate change effectively and lead their teams to thrive in an ever-changing world.

Patience and Persistence

Eagles exhibit patience and persistence in their hunting, waiting for the right moment to strike. Leaders can learn to exercise patience and persistence, understanding that success may require time and effort, and persevering towards their goals. Eagles exhibit patience and persistence in their hunting behaviors, waiting for the right moment to strike and not giving up easily. Leaders can learn from eagles' approach and apply it to their own leadership journey. Here's a detailed explanation with examples and steps on how eagles exhibit patience and persistence and how leaders can emulate it:

1. Waiting for the Right Moment: Eagles display patience in their hunting, carefully observing their prey and waiting for the opportune moment to strike. They understand the importance of timing and precision. Similarly, leaders can exercise patience by recognizing that achieving their goals may require waiting for the right moment or seizing the right opportunities. Example: Warren Buffett, one of the most successful investors in the world, exemplifies patience in his investment approach. He waits for the right opportunities to invest and holds long-term positions, demonstrating the power of patience in achieving financial success.

Steps for Leaders to Emulate:

- ✓ Define your goals and vision: Clearly define your goals and vision for your team or organization. Understand what you are working towards and the expected outcomes.

✓ Develop a strategic plan: Create a strategic plan that outlines the steps required to achieve your goals. Identify milestones and the timeline for each milestone.

✓ Practice active patience: Embrace the concept of active patience by actively working towards your goals while being patient for the right opportunities or outcomes. Continuously evaluate and adjust your strategies as needed.

✓ Monitor progress and adjust: Regularly review your progress and make adjustments to your plans or strategies as necessary. Patience does not mean being stagnant; it involves being adaptable and responsive to changing circumstances.

2. Perseverance in the Face of Challenges: Eagles exhibit persistence in their hunting pursuits. They do not give up easily and continue their efforts until they succeed. Leaders can practice persistence by staying committed to their goals, even in the face of obstacles or setbacks. Example: Oprah Winfrey, a media mogul and philanthropist, faced numerous challenges throughout her career. However, she persisted in pursuing her passion and vision, ultimately becoming one of the most influential figures in the entertainment industry.

Steps for Leaders to Emulate:

✓ Maintain a growth mindset: Cultivate a mindset that views challenges as opportunities for growth and learning. Embrace setbacks as learning experiences that can propel you forward.

- ✓ Learn from failures: Extract lessons from failures and setbacks. Use these experiences to improve your strategies and decision-making processes.
- ✓ Seek support and encouragement: Surround yourself with a support network of mentors, coaches, or trusted advisors who can provide guidance and encouragement during challenging times.
- ✓ Stay focused on the big picture: Keep your long-term goals in mind and remain focused on your vision, even when facing short-term difficulties. Remember that setbacks are temporary and can be overcome with persistence.

3. Balancing Patience and Proactivity: Eagles strike a balance between patience and proactivity in their hunting. They remain patient while observing their prey but take swift action when the opportune moment arises. Similarly, leaders can learn to balance patience and proactivity, recognizing when to wait and when to take decisive action. Example: Tim Cook, the CEO of Apple, exemplifies the balance between patience and proactivity. He maintained Apple's commitment to innovation while patiently awaiting the right timing to launch new products and enter new markets.

Steps for Leaders to Emulate:

- ✓ Assess the situation: Evaluate the circumstances and assess whether patience or proactivity is needed. Consider the potential risks, benefits, and timing of taking action.

- ✓ Set clear milestones and deadlines: Break down your goals into smaller milestones and set deadlines for each milestone. This helps to maintain a sense of progress while being patient for the right opportunities.
- ✓ Continuously evaluate the situation: Regularly review the progress towards your goals and reassess whether adjustments in strategy or timing are needed. This ensures that you remain agile and adaptable.
- ✓ Seize opportunities when they arise: When the right opportunity presents itself, be prepared to take decisive action. This requires a balance of patience, readiness, and the ability to recognize opportune moments.

4. Inspire and Motivate Others: Eagles inspire and motivate their flock through their patience and persistence in hunting. They serve as role models, instilling a sense of determination and perseverance in their young. Leaders can inspire and motivate their teams by demonstrating patience and persistence in their own actions. Example: Nelson Mandela, the former President of South Africa, exhibited extraordinary patience and persistence throughout his fight against apartheid. His unwavering commitment to justice and reconciliation inspired millions and helped bring about lasting change.

Steps for Leaders to Emulate:

- ✓ Lead by example: Demonstrate patience and persistence in your own actions and decisions.

Show resilience in the face of challenges and maintain a positive attitude.

✓ Communicate and share stories: Communicate stories of perseverance and success to inspire and motivate your team members. Highlight examples of individuals or teams who overcame obstacles through patience and persistence.

✓ Provide support and resources: Offer support and resources to help team members overcome challenges and stay motivated. Provide coaching, mentorship, or training opportunities to enhance their skills and build their resilience.

✓ Celebrate milestones and achievements: Acknowledge and celebrate individual and team achievements along the journey. Recognize and reward perseverance, reinforcing its importance in the organizational culture.

By observing how eagles exhibit patience and persistence and applying the corresponding steps, leaders can develop the mindset and behaviors necessary to navigate challenges, persevere towards their goals, and inspire their teams. By practicing patience, maintaining perseverance, balancing patience and proactivity, and inspiring others, leaders can foster a culture of resilience and achieve long-term success.

Resilience in Adversity

Eagles face adversity, such as harsh weather conditions, but remain resilient and continue their pursuits. Leaders can learn to be resilient in the face of challenges, inspiring their teams to persevere and overcome obstacles.

Eagles exhibit resilience in the face of adversity, enduring harsh weather conditions and persisting in their pursuits. Leaders can learn from eagles' resilience and apply it to their own leadership approach. Here's a detailed explanation with examples and steps on how eagles exhibit resilience in adversity and how leaders can emulate it:

1. Enduring Harsh Conditions: Eagles face harsh weather conditions, including storms and extreme temperatures, yet they persevere in their pursuits. They adapt their behaviors and strategies to navigate through these challenges. Similarly, leaders should demonstrate resilience by staying committed to their goals and finding ways to overcome obstacles, even in the face of adversity. Example: Sir Ernest Shackleton, a renowned polar explorer, displayed exceptional resilience during the ill-fated Endurance expedition. Despite being stranded in the Antarctic due to the ship's loss, Shackleton and his crew displayed resilience and determination, eventually surviving and returning home.

Steps for Leaders to Emulate:
- ✓ Foster a resilient mindset: Cultivate a mindset that sees challenges as opportunities for

growth and learning. Encourage team members to view setbacks as temporary and seek solutions to overcome them.

- ✓ Stay focused on the vision: Maintain clarity and focus on the long-term vision, even when facing adversity. Communicate the vision to the team and reinforce its importance, helping them remain motivated and resilient.
- ✓ Encourage open communication: Create an environment where team members can openly express their concerns, fears, and challenges. Encourage open dialogue and provide support to address their needs.
- ✓ Adapt strategies and approaches: Assess the situation and adapt strategies and approaches as needed to navigate through challenges. Encourage flexibility and creativity in finding alternative solutions.

2. Persevering in the Face of Setbacks: Eagles encounter setbacks in their hunting endeavors, such as unsuccessful attempts to catch prey. However, they persist and continue their pursuit until they achieve success. Leaders can exhibit perseverance in the face of setbacks, inspiring their teams to overcome obstacles and keep striving for their goals. Example: J.K. Rowling, the author of the Harry Potter series, faced numerous rejections before finding a publisher. Despite setbacks, she persevered in her writing and eventually achieved immense success, becoming one of the best-selling authors in history.

Steps for Leaders to Emulate:

- ✓ Set realistic expectations: Help team members understand that setbacks and challenges are a normal part of the journey. Set realistic expectations and encourage a mindset that values resilience and perseverance.
- ✓ Provide support and resources: Offer support and resources to help team members overcome setbacks. This can include coaching, mentoring, training, or providing additional tools or resources needed to overcome challenges.
- ✓ Encourage a learning mindset: Emphasize the importance of learning from setbacks and using them as opportunities for growth. Encourage team members to reflect on their experiences, extract lessons learned, and apply those insights to future endeavors.
- ✓ Celebrate small wins: Acknowledge and celebrate small victories along the way. Recognize the efforts and progress made, even if the ultimate goal has not yet been achieved. This helps boost morale and encourages perseverance.

3. Adapting to Change: Eagles demonstrate adaptability by adjusting their hunting strategies and flight patterns to changing circumstances. They remain agile in the face of unexpected events or shifts in their environment. Leaders should exhibit adaptability and encourage their teams to embrace change as a means of resilience. Example: Reed Hastings, the co-founder and CEO of Netflix, led the company through a significant shift from DVD rentals to online streaming. By adapting to the changing media

landscape and consumer preferences, Netflix emerged as a dominant player in the entertainment industry.

Steps for Leaders to Emulate:

- ✓ Encourage flexibility and agility: Foster a culture that values flexibility and agility in responding to change. Encourage team members to embrace new ideas, challenge the status quo, and adapt their strategies when necessary.
- ✓ Promote continuous learning: Emphasize the importance of continuous learning and personal growth. Encourage team members to acquire new skills, stay updated with industry trends, and be open to learning from others.
- ✓ Develop contingency plans: Anticipate potential challenges or changes and develop contingency plans. This allows the team to respond quickly and effectively to unexpected events or shifting circumstances.
- ✓ Communicate the purpose behind change: Clearly communicate the reasons and benefits of any required changes to the team. Help them understand how the changes align with the organization's goals and values.

4. Provide Support and Encouragement: Eagles exhibit resilience within their flock, providing support and encouragement to one another. Leaders can emulate this by fostering a supportive environment where team members feel empowered, motivated, and united in overcoming adversity. Example: Mary Barra, the CEO of General Motors, faced significant challenges in steering the company through recalls and reputation issues. She fostered

resilience within the organization by providing support, empowering employees, and focusing on a culture of transparency and accountability.

Steps for Leaders to Emulate:

- ✓ Foster open communication: Create an environment where open and transparent communication is encouraged. Actively listen to team members' concerns, provide guidance, and address their needs.
- ✓ Offer mentorship and coaching: Provide mentorship and coaching to support the development of resilience in team members. Share personal experiences and lessons learned to inspire and guide them through adversity.
- ✓ Encourage peer support: Foster a culture of support and collaboration among team members. Encourage them to provide assistance and encouragement to one another, promoting a sense of unity and shared responsibility.
- ✓ Recognize and celebrate resilience: Acknowledge and celebrate instances where team members demonstrate resilience in the face of adversity. Recognize their efforts and provide positive reinforcement for their resilience and perseverance.

By observing how eagles exhibit resilience in adversity and applying the corresponding steps, leaders can develop their own resilience and inspire their teams to persevere through challenges. By fostering a resilient mindset, persevering in the face of setbacks, adapting to change, and providing support and encouragement, leaders can create an environment that embraces resilience and achieves success even in the most challenging circumstances.

Innovation and Creativity

Eagles exhibit innovative hunting techniques, adapting their strategies to capture prey. Leaders can learn to foster a culture of innovation and creativity, encouraging their teams to think outside the box and find new solutions to problems.

Eagles exhibit innovation and creativity in their hunting techniques, adapting their strategies to capture prey effectively. Leaders can learn from eagles' approach and apply it to foster a culture of innovation and creativity within their organizations. Here's a detailed explanation with examples and steps on how eagles exhibit innovation and creativity, and how leaders can emulate it:

1. Adapting Hunting Techniques: Eagles showcase innovation by adapting their hunting techniques to suit different prey and environments. They experiment with different approaches, such as aerial dives or cooperative hunting, to increase their success rates. Similarly, leaders can foster innovation by encouraging their teams to adapt and experiment with new approaches to problem-solving and decision-making. Example: SpaceX, led by Elon Musk, revolutionized the space industry by developing reusable rockets. Their innovative approach of landing and reusing rockets significantly reduced the cost of space exploration and opened up new possibilities for the industry.

Steps for Leaders to Emulate:

✓ Encourage a culture of curiosity: Foster a culture that encourages curiosity and

questioning the status quo. Create an environment where team members feel comfortable exploring new ideas and challenging conventional thinking.
- ✓ Provide resources for experimentation: Allocate resources, time, and support for teams to experiment and test new ideas. Encourage a mindset that sees failures as valuable learning experiences.
- ✓ Reward and recognize innovation: Celebrate and reward individuals and teams who demonstrate innovative thinking and generate impactful ideas. This reinforces the value placed on innovation within the organization.
- ✓ Encourage cross-functional collaboration: Facilitate collaboration across teams and departments to foster the exchange of diverse perspectives and ideas. Encourage employees to seek input from different areas of expertise to generate innovative solutions.
2. Embracing New Technologies: Eagles adapt their hunting strategies by leveraging their physical abilities and utilizing their keen eyesight. Similarly, leaders can foster innovation by embracing new technologies and encouraging their teams to explore and adopt cutting-edge tools and techniques. Example: Apple, under the leadership of Steve Jobs, disrupted multiple industries by introducing innovative products such as the iPod, iPhone, and iPad. Their ability to leverage emerging technologies and create seamless user experiences transformed the way we consume media and communicate.

Steps for Leaders to Emulate:

- ✓ Stay informed about emerging technologies: Keep up-to-date with technological advancements relevant to your industry. Attend conferences, engage in industry forums, and encourage team members to share insights on new technologies.
- ✓ Foster a learning culture: Encourage continuous learning and professional development, particularly in areas related to emerging technologies. Provide training opportunities and allocate time for employees to stay updated.
- ✓ Provide resources and support: Invest in necessary technologies, tools, and infrastructure to enable teams to experiment and innovate. Remove barriers that may hinder the adoption of new technologies.
- ✓ Empower innovation champions: Identify individuals within the organization who have a passion for innovation and empower them to lead and drive innovative initiatives. Encourage others to learn from their experiences and embrace innovation.

3. Encouraging Diverse Perspectives: Eagles exhibit creativity in their hunting strategies by considering various factors, such as wind patterns, prey behavior, and environmental conditions. Leaders can foster creativity by encouraging diverse perspectives and seeking input from team members with different backgrounds, experiences, and expertise. Example: IDEO, a renowned design and innovation firm, has a culture that encourages cross-disciplinary collaboration and diversity of thought. By bringing together individuals from

diverse backgrounds, they generate creative solutions for their clients.

Steps for Leaders to Emulate:

- ✓ Build diverse teams: Assemble teams with diverse backgrounds, skills, and perspectives. Foster an inclusive environment where everyone's contributions are valued and respected.
- ✓ Facilitate brainstorming sessions: Conduct structured brainstorming sessions to encourage idea generation. Provide a safe space where team members feel comfortable sharing their thoughts and suggestions.
- ✓ Encourage exploration of multiple solutions: Encourage teams to explore multiple solutions to a problem. Emphasize that creativity thrives when multiple perspectives are considered and evaluated.
- ✓ Provide autonomy and freedom: Give teams the autonomy to explore innovative ideas and experiment with new approaches. Encourage risk-taking and create an environment where failures are seen as learning opportunities.

4. Promote a Growth Mindset: Eagles exhibit innovation by continuously learning and adapting their hunting techniques. Leaders can foster a growth mindset within their teams, encouraging them to embrace challenges, learn from failures, and continuously improve. Example: Google's "20% time" policy allowed employees to spend a portion of their workweek on projects of personal interest. This policy led to the creation of innovative products and services such as Gmail and Google Maps.

Steps for Leaders to Emulate:
- ✓ Foster a safe environment for experimentation: Create an environment where employees feel safe to experiment, take risks, and share their ideas without fear of judgment or negative consequences.
- ✓ Encourage continuous learning: Support and provide resources for professional development. Offer training programs, workshops, or opportunities for employees to gain new skills and knowledge.
- ✓ Recognize and reward innovation: Acknowledge and reward employees who demonstrate innovative thinking, take initiative, and contribute to the organization's success. Celebrate both big and small wins.
- ✓ Encourage cross-pollination of ideas: Promote knowledge sharing and collaboration across teams and departments. Encourage employees to share insights, experiences, and lessons learned to inspire innovation throughout the organization.

By observing how eagles exhibit innovation and creativity and applying the corresponding steps, leaders can foster a culture of innovation within their organizations. By encouraging adaptation, embracing new technologies, encouraging diverse perspectives, and promoting a growth mindset, leaders can inspire their teams to think outside the box, generate new ideas, and find innovative solutions to challenges.

Empathy and Emotional Intelligence

Eagles exhibit empathy within their flock, showing care for their young and cooperating with their mates. Leaders can learn to possess empathy and emotional intelligence, understanding and connecting with their team members on a deeper level.

Eagles exhibit empathy within their flock, demonstrating care and cooperation towards their young and mates. They showcase emotional intelligence by understanding the needs and emotions of their fellow eagles. Leaders can learn from eagles' behavior and apply empathy and emotional intelligence to build strong connections with their team members. Here's a detailed explanation with examples and steps on how eagles exhibit empathy and emotional intelligence, and how leaders can emulate it:

1. Caring for the Young: Eagles exhibit empathy by nurturing and caring for their young. They protect their offspring, provide food, and teach them essential skills for survival. Similarly, leaders can demonstrate empathy by genuinely caring for the well-being and development of their team members. Example: Indra Nooyi, former CEO of PepsiCo, prioritized the well-being and professional growth of her employees. She implemented initiatives such as the "Performance with Purpose" program, which aimed to enhance employees' lives and create a supportive work environment.

Steps for Leaders to Emulate:

✓ Develop genuine connections: Build meaningful relationships with team members based on trust, respect, and open communication. Show a genuine interest in their well-being, both personally and professionally.

✓ Practice active listening: Listen attentively to team members, allowing them to express their thoughts, concerns, and ideas. Demonstrate empathy by acknowledging their perspectives and validating their feelings.

✓ Provide support and resources: Understand the individual needs and aspirations of team members. Offer support, mentorship, and resources to help them achieve their goals and overcome challenges.

✓ Create a positive work environment: Foster a positive and inclusive work environment where team members feel valued, supported, and safe to express themselves. Encourage collaboration and mutual support among team members.

2. Cooperating with Mates: Eagles exhibit empathy by cooperating with their mates in raising their young and maintaining their territory. They work together, communicate effectively, and share responsibilities. Leaders can display empathy by fostering collaboration, effective communication, and shared responsibilities among team members. Example: Larry Page and Sergey Brin, the co-founders of Google, worked collaboratively to build a culture of innovation and collaboration within the company. They emphasized the importance of teamwork and fostered an

environment where ideas and expertise were shared freely.

Steps for Leaders to Emulate:

- ✓ Promote a collaborative culture: Encourage collaboration and teamwork within the organization. Create opportunities for team members to work together on projects, share ideas, and leverage each other's strengths.
- ✓ Foster effective communication: Promote open and transparent communication among team members. Encourage active listening, constructive feedback, and the sharing of ideas and information.
- ✓ Encourage diverse perspectives: Value and encourage diverse perspectives and opinions within the team. Create an inclusive environment where everyone feels comfortable expressing their thoughts and ideas.
- ✓ Share responsibilities: Foster a sense of shared ownership and accountability among team members. Encourage individuals to support and help each other, promoting a collective sense of success.

3. Understanding Emotions and Needs: Eagles exhibit emotional intelligence by understanding the emotions and needs of their fellow eagles. They can sense distress, danger, or signals from their mates, and respond accordingly. Leaders can develop emotional intelligence by understanding and empathizing with the emotions, needs, and motivations of their team members. Example: Satya Nadella, the CEO of Microsoft, has emphasized the importance of empathy and

emotional intelligence in leadership. He introduced initiatives to cultivate a culture of empathy within the organization, focusing on understanding customers and employees at a deeper level.

Steps for Leaders to Emulate:

- ✓ Cultivate self-awareness: Develop self-awareness by reflecting on your own emotions, strengths, weaknesses, and triggers. Understand how your emotions and behaviors can impact others.
- ✓ Practice empathy: Put yourself in others' shoes and strive to understand their perspectives, feelings, and needs. Demonstrate empathy by considering their emotions and experiences when making decisions or providing feedback.
- ✓ Encourage emotional expression: Create an environment where team members feel comfortable expressing their emotions and concerns. Encourage open dialogue and provide a safe space for individuals to share their thoughts and feelings.
- ✓ Tailor leadership approaches: Adapt your leadership style and communication to meet the unique needs and preferences of individual team members. Recognize and appreciate diversity in personalities, working styles, and motivations.
4. Developing Emotional Resilience: Eagles exhibit emotional resilience by remaining focused and composed during challenging situations. They maintain their purpose and continue their pursuits despite setbacks or disturbances. Leaders can cultivate emotional

resilience within themselves and support their team members in developing resilience. Example: Sheryl Sandberg, the COO of Facebook, has been an advocate for building emotional resilience in the face of adversity. Through her book "Option B," she shares her personal journey and provides strategies for resilience after the loss of her husband.

Steps for Leaders to Emulate:

- ✓ Foster a growth mindset: Encourage a growth mindset that views challenges as opportunities for growth and learning. Help team members see setbacks as temporary and encourage them to persist and learn from failures.

- ✓ Provide support and resources: Offer support mechanisms such as coaching, mentoring, or access to resources that can help individuals build emotional resilience. Provide opportunities for learning and personal development.

- ✓ Lead by example: Demonstrate emotional resilience in your own actions and reactions. Show composure and optimism during challenging times, inspiring others to do the same.

- ✓ Celebrate resilience: Recognize and celebrate instances where team members demonstrate emotional resilience in the face of challenges. Highlight and reward their efforts and achievements.

By observing how eagles exhibit empathy and emotional intelligence and applying the corresponding steps, leaders can cultivate a culture of empathy, emotional intelligence, and resilience within their organizations. By caring for their team members, promoting cooperation, understanding emotions, and developing emotional resilience, leaders can create an environment where individuals feel valued, supported, and empowered to thrive.

Ethical Decision-Making

Eagles exhibit ethical behavior within their social structure, respecting boundaries and exhibiting fairness. Leaders can learn to make ethical decisions, aligning their actions with values and promoting a culture of integrity within their organizations.

Eagles exhibit ethical behavior within their social structure, demonstrating respect for boundaries and fairness. They establish and maintain territories while adhering to rules and hierarchies. Leaders can learn from eagles' ethical behavior and apply it to make ethical decisions and promote a culture of integrity within their organizations. Here's a detailed explanation with examples and steps on how eagles exhibit ethical decision-making and how leaders can emulate it:

1. Respect for Boundaries: Eagles exhibit respect for boundaries within their territories, recognizing and adhering to the established limits. They respect the boundaries of other eagles and avoid encroaching upon their territories. Similarly, leaders can demonstrate respect for boundaries by recognizing and honoring the boundaries of individuals and teams within the organization. Example: Patagonia, an outdoor clothing company, is known for its ethical practices and commitment to environmental stewardship. The company respects the boundaries of the environment and implements sustainable manufacturing processes to minimize its ecological footprint.

Steps for Leaders to Emulate:
- ✓ Clearly define expectations and boundaries: Establish clear expectations, guidelines, and boundaries for individuals and teams within the organization. Ensure that these boundaries align with ethical principles and values.
- ✓ Foster a culture of respect: Promote a culture of respect and inclusion, where team members are encouraged to respect the boundaries, opinions, and perspectives of others. Encourage open dialogue and healthy collaboration.
- ✓ Lead by example: Demonstrate respect for boundaries in your own actions and decisions. Avoid micromanaging, honor personal time and space, and respect the privacy and confidentiality of individuals.
- ✓ Address boundary violations: Address any instances where boundaries are crossed or violated promptly and appropriately. Provide guidance and support to help individuals understand and respect the boundaries set within the organization.
2. Fairness and Justice: Eagles exhibit fairness and justice within their social structure. They establish hierarchies and demonstrate fairness in distributing resources and protecting their flock. Similarly, leaders can promote fairness and justice by making decisions that are consistent, unbiased, and equitable. Example: Ben & Jerry's, an ice cream company, is known for its commitment to social justice and equity. The company actively works to address systemic

inequalities, pays fair wages to its employees, and supports causes related to social and environmental justice.

Steps for Leaders to Emulate:

- ✓ Establish fair policies and procedures: Develop fair and transparent policies and procedures that guide decision-making within the organization. Ensure that these policies promote equality, diversity, and inclusion.
- ✓ Encourage diversity and inclusion: Foster a diverse and inclusive work environment where individuals are valued and treated fairly, regardless of their background or identity. Encourage diverse perspectives and ensure equal opportunities for growth and advancement.
- ✓ Practice unbiased decision-making: Make decisions based on objective criteria and avoid favoritism or bias. Consider multiple viewpoints and gather relevant data before making important decisions.
- ✓ Promote ethical behavior: Set the tone for ethical behavior by modeling fairness and justice in your own actions. Recognize and reward individuals who exhibit fairness, integrity, and ethical behavior.

3. Alignment with Core Values: Eagles exhibit ethical behavior that is aligned with their instincts and survival as a species. They follow their natural instincts and adhere to their biological roles within the flock. Similarly, leaders can align their decisions and actions with the core values and purpose of the organization. Example: TOMS, a footwear company, operates with a "One for One"

business model, where for every pair of shoes sold, a pair is donated to a person in need. This model reflects the company's core values of giving back and making a positive impact on society.

Steps for Leaders to Emulate:
- ✓ Define and communicate core values: Clearly define the core values of the organization and communicate them effectively to all team members. Ensure that these values guide decision-making and behaviors across the organization.
- ✓ Regularly evaluate alignment: Continuously assess the alignment between decisions, actions, and the organization's core values. Regularly review and reflect on whether decisions align with the desired ethical standards.
- ✓ Encourage ethical discussions: Create opportunities for team members to engage in discussions about ethics and values. Encourage open dialogue and provide platforms for employees to express their perspectives and concerns.
- ✓ Provide ethical training and support: Offer training programs that focus on ethical decision-making and provide resources to support individuals in making ethical choices. Offer guidance and mentorship for individuals facing ethical dilemmas.

4. Encourage Ethical Courage: Eagles exhibit ethical courage by defending their territories and protecting their flock from external threats. Leaders can promote ethical courage by encouraging team members to speak up,

question unethical practices, and take a stand for what is right. Example: Whistleblowers, such as Sherron Watkins of Enron and Edward Snowden of NSA, demonstrated ethical courage by exposing illegal or unethical activities within their organizations.

Steps for Leaders to Emulate:
- ✓ Create a safe and supportive environment: Foster an environment where team members feel safe to express their concerns and raise ethical issues without fear of retaliation. Encourage open and honest communication.
- ✓ Lead with integrity: Demonstrate ethical behavior and lead by example. Encourage transparency, honesty, and accountability within the organization.
- ✓ Establish channels for reporting: Implement mechanisms for reporting ethical concerns or violations anonymously and without fear of reprisal. Ensure that these channels are well-communicated and easily accessible to all team members.
- ✓ Reward ethical behavior: Recognize and reward individuals who exhibit ethical courage and uphold the organization's values. Celebrate instances where team members speak up or take actions aligned with ethical principles.

By observing how eagles exhibit ethical decision-making and applying the corresponding steps, leaders can cultivate a culture of integrity, fairness, and ethical behavior within their organizations. By respecting boundaries, promoting fairness and justice, aligning decisions with core values, and encouraging ethical courage, leaders can inspire their teams to make ethical decisions and contribute to a positive and ethical work environment.

Flexibility and Adaptation

Eagles are flexible in their flight patterns, adapting to changing wind currents. Leaders can learn to be flexible and adaptive in their approaches, adjusting strategies and embracing change to stay ahead in dynamic markets.

Eagles exhibit flexibility and adaptation in their flight patterns, adjusting to changing wind currents to optimize their flight and conserve energy. Leaders can learn from eagles' flexibility and apply it to their leadership approach. Here's a detailed explanation with examples and steps on how eagles exhibit flexibility and adaptation, and how leaders can emulate it:

1. Adjusting to Changing Wind Currents: Eagles demonstrate flexibility by adjusting their flight patterns in response to changing wind currents. They adapt their wingspan and position to optimize their flight efficiency and conserve energy. Similarly, leaders can exhibit flexibility by adjusting their strategies and approaches in response to changing market dynamics and emerging opportunities. Example: Amazon, under the leadership of Jeff Bezos, initially focused on online book sales but demonstrated flexibility by adapting its business model to become the world's largest online retailer, offering a wide range of products and services.

Steps for Leaders to Emulate:
- ✓ Stay informed and anticipate changes: Stay abreast of industry trends, market shifts, and emerging technologies. Anticipate changes

and proactively seek opportunities to adapt and innovate.

- ✓ Foster a culture of flexibility: Encourage a culture that embraces change and agility. Create an environment where team members are open to new ideas and are encouraged to explore different approaches to problem-solving and decision-making.
- ✓ Encourage collaboration and diverse perspectives: Foster collaboration and seek input from diverse perspectives within the organization. Encourage team members to share their ideas and viewpoints, fostering a collective effort in adapting to change.
- ✓ Empower employees to make decisions: Provide autonomy and empower employees to make decisions and take appropriate actions in response to changing circumstances. Encourage them to be proactive and embrace flexibility in their roles.

2. Embracing Change: Eagles embrace change by adjusting their flight patterns, migration routes, and hunting strategies based on factors such as weather, prey availability, and environmental conditions. Leaders can emulate this by embracing change and encouraging their teams to be adaptable and agile in responding to new challenges and opportunities. Example: Microsoft, led by Satya Nadella, shifted its focus from traditional software licensing to a cloud-based subscription model, embracing the changing landscape of technology and responding to customer demands.

Steps for Leaders to Emulate:

- ✓ Communicate the importance of adaptability: Emphasize the importance of being adaptable and embracing change within the organization. Communicate the rationale behind changes and the benefits they bring to the team and the organization as a whole.
- ✓ Provide resources for learning and development: Invest in training and development programs to enhance the skills and knowledge of team members. Equip them with the tools and resources needed to adapt to new technologies and changing market demands.
- ✓ Encourage experimentation and risk-taking: Create an environment that encourages experimentation and risk-taking. Provide support for pilot projects and encourage teams to test new ideas and approaches.
- ✓ Foster resilience and agility: Help team members develop resilience and agility in navigating change. Provide guidance and support to help them adapt to new circumstances and overcome challenges.

3. Agile Decision-Making: Eagles exhibit agility in decision-making, swiftly adjusting their flight paths and hunting strategies based on real-time observations and changing conditions. Leaders can adopt an agile decision-making approach, quickly gathering relevant information, assessing options, and making informed decisions in response to changing circumstances. Example: Netflix, led by Reed Hastings, transformed its business model from DVD rentals to online streaming by quickly

adapting to the changing landscape of media consumption and consumer preferences.

Steps for Leaders to Emulate:

- ✓ Foster a culture of agility: Establish a culture that values agility and quick decision-making. Encourage team members to gather relevant information efficiently and make decisions promptly.
- ✓ Promote cross-functional collaboration: Encourage collaboration across teams and departments to facilitate faster decision-making. Foster an environment where diverse perspectives can be shared and considered.
- ✓ Develop a framework for rapid decision-making: Implement a decision-making framework that enables quick assessments and evaluation of options. Define decision criteria and empower team members to make decisions within their respective areas of responsibility.
- ✓ Encourage continuous learning and feedback: Promote a culture of continuous learning and improvement. Encourage team members to learn from the outcomes of their decisions, provide feedback, and iterate their approaches.

4. Embrace Technology and Innovation: Eagles leverage their natural abilities to adapt to changing conditions. Leaders can emulate this by embracing technology and innovation, using them as tools to facilitate flexibility and adaptation in their organizations. Example: Tesla, led by Elon Musk, disrupted the automotive industry by embracing electric vehicles and autonomous driving technology.

They continuously innovate and adapt to advancements in technology and market demands.

Steps for Leaders to Emulate:
- ✓ Stay informed about technological advancements: Keep abreast of emerging technologies and their potential impact on the industry. Encourage team members to explore and understand the possibilities offered by new technologies.
- ✓ Foster innovation and creativity: Create an environment that encourages innovation and creativity. Provide resources, support, and dedicated time for teams to experiment with new technologies and explore innovative solutions.
- ✓ Encourage collaboration with technology experts: Foster collaboration between the organization and external technology experts, such as startups or research institutions. Collaborative efforts can provide insights into emerging technologies and potential applications.
- ✓ Invest in technology infrastructure and training- Invest in technology infrastructure and provide training opportunities to ensure that employees have the necessary skills and knowledge to leverage technology effectively.
- ✓ Encourage a mindset of continuous improvement: Foster a culture that values continuous improvement and encourages employees to proactively identify opportunities for leveraging technology to enhance flexibility and adaptation.

By observing how eagles exhibit flexibility and adaptation and applying the corresponding steps, leaders can foster a culture of agility, innovation, and resilience within their organizations. By staying informed, embracing change, adopting agile decision-making approaches, and leveraging technology and innovation, leaders can position their organizations to successfully navigate and thrive in dynamic and evolving markets.

Strategic Partnerships

Eagles form partnerships during their mating season, cooperating and working together. Leaders can learn to develop strategic partnerships, leveraging synergies and collaborating with other organizations to drive growth and success.

Eagles exhibit strategic partnerships during their mating season, where they cooperate and work together with their mates to ensure the survival and growth of their offspring. Leaders can learn from eagles' approach to strategic partnerships and apply it to their leadership practices. Here's a detailed explanation with examples and steps on how eagles exhibit strategic partnerships and how leaders can emulate it:

1. Cooperative Mating Season: Eagles form strategic partnerships during their mating season, working collaboratively with their mates to build nests, incubate eggs, and raise their young. They share responsibilities and cooperate to ensure the success of their offspring. Similarly, leaders can foster strategic partnerships by collaborating with other organizations to achieve shared goals and drive growth. Example: The partnership between Apple and Nike, known as Nike+iPod, brought together Apple's technology and Nike's athletic expertise to create a fitness tracking system for runners. This collaboration leveraged the strengths of both companies to deliver a unique and innovative product.

Steps for Leaders to Emulate:

- ✓ Identify shared goals and values: Seek out organizations that share similar goals, values, or complementary capabilities. Look for potential partners who can enhance your products, services, or market reach.
- ✓ Build trust and rapport: Develop strong relationships with potential partners based on trust, mutual respect, and open communication. Invest time and effort in building a foundation of trust before entering into formal partnerships.
- ✓ Define clear objectives and roles: Clearly define the objectives and expectations of the partnership. Determine the specific roles and responsibilities of each organization to ensure alignment and accountability.
- ✓ Foster open communication: Establish open channels of communication between the partnering organizations. Encourage regular communication and collaboration to ensure that both parties stay informed and engaged throughout the partnership.
- ✓ Leverage complementary strengths: Identify the unique strengths and capabilities that each organization brings to the partnership. Leverage these complementary strengths to drive innovation, improve operational efficiency, or access new markets.
- ✓ Share resources and expertise: Explore opportunities to share resources, knowledge, and expertise. This could include joint marketing efforts, shared research and development initiatives, or cross-training programs.

- ✓ Monitor and evaluate the partnership: Regularly monitor and evaluate the progress and impact of the partnership. Assess whether the partnership is achieving its intended goals and make adjustments as needed.
- ✓ Nurture long-term relationships: Treat the partnership as a long-term commitment. Invest in maintaining and nurturing the relationship with your strategic partners, fostering mutual growth and success.

2. Industry Alliances: Eagles exhibit a form of industry alliance by congregating and soaring together in thermal updrafts, benefiting from the collective energy and guidance. Leaders can emulate this by forming industry alliances or collaborations to leverage collective knowledge, resources, and market influence. Example: The airline industry's establishment of airline alliances, such as Star Alliance and SkyTeam, enables member airlines to expand their reach, provide seamless travel experiences, and share resources and benefits.

Steps for Leaders to Emulate:
- ✓ Identify industry partners: Identify potential partners within your industry who have complementary strengths, products, or services. Look for organizations that can help you enhance your market presence, access new customers, or expand your offerings.
- ✓ Establish common goals: Define common goals and objectives for the alliance. Ensure that all participating organizations have a shared understanding of the purpose and desired outcomes of the collaboration.

- ✓ Define collaboration framework: Establish a framework that outlines the structure, governance, and decision-making processes of the alliance. Determine how resources, risks, and benefits will be shared among the partners.
- ✓ Foster collaboration and knowledge sharing: Encourage collaboration and knowledge sharing among alliance members. Facilitate regular meetings, workshops, or conferences where partners can exchange ideas, best practices, and market insights.
- ✓ Align branding and marketing efforts: Coordinate branding and marketing efforts among alliance members to create a cohesive and compelling message to customers. Leverage the collective reach and influence of the alliance to enhance market visibility.
- ✓ Collaborate on research and innovation: Explore opportunities for joint research and innovation initiatives. Pool resources, knowledge, and expertise to address industry challenges, develop new technologies, or create innovative solutions.
- ✓ Monitor and review alliance performance: Regularly assess the performance and impact of the alliance. Monitor key metrics, such as customer satisfaction, market share, or revenue growth, to evaluate the effectiveness of the collaboration and make adjustments as necessary.
- ✓ Seek continuous improvement: Continuously seek ways to improve the alliance and maximize its value for all participating organizations. Encourage feedback from

alliance members and implement changes to enhance collaboration and outcomes.

By observing how eagles exhibit strategic partnerships and applying the corresponding steps, leaders can foster effective collaborations, leverage synergies, and drive growth and success. By identifying shared goals, building trust, fostering open communication, and leveraging complementary strengths, leaders can develop strategic partnerships that deliver mutual benefits and create value for all involved parties.

Continuous Improvement

Eagles continually refine their hunting techniques, seeking improvement with each experience. Leaders can learn to prioritize continuous improvement, fostering a culture of learning and development within their teams and organizations.

Eagles exhibit continuous improvement in their hunting techniques, constantly refining their skills and strategies to become more efficient and successful. They learn from each hunting experience and apply that knowledge to improve their future performance. Leaders can learn from eagles' approach to continuous improvement and apply it to their leadership practices. Here's a detailed explanation with examples and steps on how eagles exhibit continuous improvement, and how leaders can emulate it:

1. Learning from Experience: Eagles learn from their hunting experiences, analyzing what worked and what didn't, and adjusting their strategies accordingly. They continually refine their techniques to become more effective in capturing prey. Similarly, leaders can encourage their teams to learn from experiences and reflect on both successes and failures. Example: Toyota, renowned for its continuous improvement approach, implemented the "Toyota Production System" (TPS) that encourages employees at all levels to identify and address problems to improve efficiency and quality.

Steps for Leaders to Emulate:

- ✓ Create a learning culture: Foster a culture of continuous learning and improvement within the organization. Encourage employees to view mistakes and failures as learning opportunities and provide support for personal and professional development.
- ✓ Encourage reflection: Encourage team members to reflect on their experiences and identify lessons learned. Foster an environment where individuals feel comfortable sharing their insights and suggestions for improvement.
- ✓ Conduct after-action reviews: Conduct structured after-action reviews following projects, initiatives, or significant milestones. Encourage team members to identify successes, challenges, and areas for improvement. Use these insights to refine processes and enhance future performance.
- ✓ Share knowledge and best practices: Facilitate knowledge sharing among team members. Encourage the documentation and dissemination of best practices, lessons learned, and success stories. Provide platforms for sharing experiences and insights across teams and departments.
- ✓ Encourage experimentation and innovation: Create opportunities for experimentation and innovation within the organization. Encourage individuals and teams to test new approaches, technologies, or processes. Celebrate and reward innovation and successful experiments.
- ✓ Provide training and development opportunities: Invest in training programs and

professional development opportunities to enhance the skills and knowledge of team members. Provide resources and support for individuals to acquire new competencies and stay updated on industry trends.

✓ Implement feedback mechanisms: Establish feedback mechanisms, such as performance evaluations, 360-degree feedback, or regular check-ins, to provide constructive feedback and guidance for improvement. Encourage open and honest communication about areas for growth and development.

✓ Set measurable goals: Set clear and measurable goals for individuals and teams. Regularly review progress towards these goals and provide feedback on performance. Use the goal-setting process as a means to drive continuous improvement.

✓ Recognize and reward improvement efforts: Recognize and reward individuals and teams that demonstrate a commitment to continuous improvement. Celebrate milestones, achievements, and efforts to enhance performance and drive innovation.

2. Embracing Kaizen: Kaizen is a Japanese term for continuous improvement and is often associated with the Toyota Production System. It emphasizes the idea that small, incremental changes can lead to significant improvements over time. Leaders can adopt the principles of kaizen to drive continuous improvement within their teams and organizations. Example: Amazon implements kaizen principles in its operations by continually seeking ways to improve its

logistics, supply chain, and customer experience. It encourages employees to suggest small improvements and implements those that have a positive impact on efficiency and customer satisfaction.

Steps for Leaders to Emulate:

- ✓ Emphasize small, incremental improvements: Encourage team members to identify small improvements that can be made on a regular basis. Foster a mindset that values and recognizes the impact of these incremental changes over time.
- ✓ Involve employees at all levels: Encourage employees at all levels to participate in the continuous improvement process. Empower them to identify areas for improvement and provide suggestions for change. Foster a sense of ownership and accountability for driving improvement.
- ✓ Create improvement teams: Form cross-functional improvement teams that focus on specific areas or processes. Empower these teams to analyze current practices, identify improvement opportunities, and implement changes. Provide the necessary resources and support to execute improvement initiatives.
- ✓ Implement visual management: Use visual management techniques, such as performance dashboards, Kanban boards, or process maps, to make progress and improvement visible to all. This promotes transparency and accountability for continuous improvement efforts.

- ✓ Promote open communication: Create an environment where individuals feel comfortable sharing their ideas, challenges, and improvement suggestions. Encourage open dialogue, active listening, and constructive feedback. Foster a culture where continuous improvement is a shared responsibility.
- ✓ Regularly review and celebrate improvements: Regularly review the impact of improvement initiatives and celebrate successes. Recognize and reward individuals and teams for their contributions to the continuous improvement efforts. This reinforces the importance of the process and encourages a culture of ongoing improvement.

By observing how eagles exhibit continuous improvement and applying the corresponding steps, leaders can foster a culture of learning, innovation, and growth within their teams and organizations. By encouraging reflection, learning from experiences, embracing kaizen principles, and providing the necessary support for training and development, leaders can drive continuous improvement, enhance performance, and stay ahead in a rapidly evolving business landscape.

Courage and Boldness

Eagles exhibit courage and boldness in their hunting endeavors, taking risks to secure their prey. Leaders can learn to be courageous and bold, taking calculated risks and seizing opportunities to drive innovation and growth.

Eagles exhibit courage and boldness in their hunting endeavors, taking calculated risks to secure their prey. They demonstrate fearlessness and determination, even in challenging situations. Leaders can learn from eagles' courage and boldness and apply it to their leadership practices. Here's a detailed explanation with examples and steps on how eagles exhibit courage and boldness, and how leaders can emulate it:

1. Taking Calculated Risks: Eagles take calculated risks during their hunting expeditions. They assess the situation, evaluate the potential rewards, and make decisions accordingly. They are willing to step out of their comfort zone to pursue their prey, understanding that taking risks is essential for success. Leaders can learn to take calculated risks by evaluating opportunities, weighing potential outcomes, and making informed decisions. Example: Elon Musk, the CEO of SpaceX and Tesla, has demonstrated courage and boldness by investing in groundbreaking technologies such as electric vehicles, reusable rockets, and the colonization of Mars. These ventures involve calculated risks but have the potential for significant impact and innovation.

Steps for Leaders to Emulate:
- ✓ Evaluate potential risks and rewards: Assess the potential risks and rewards associated with an opportunity or decision. Consider the potential impact on the organization, customers, and stakeholders.
- ✓ Gather information and insights: Gather relevant information, conduct research, and seek expert opinions to make informed decisions. Understand the potential challenges and opportunities that lie ahead.
- ✓ Analyze the cost of inaction: Consider the cost of not taking action and the potential missed opportunities. Evaluate the potential consequences of staying in the comfort zone and being too risk-averse.
- ✓ Foster a culture of calculated risk-taking: Create an environment where calculated risk-taking is encouraged and rewarded. Encourage team members to share innovative ideas and take calculated risks to drive growth and innovation.
- ✓ Encourage experimentation and learning: Provide support and resources for experimentation and learning. Encourage team members to explore new ideas, test hypotheses, and learn from failures to drive improvement and innovation.
- ✓ Develop contingency plans: Mitigate potential risks by developing contingency plans and considering alternative courses of action. This helps reduce uncertainty and provides a safety net in case the risk does not yield the desired outcome.

- ✓ Learn from failures: Encourage a growth mindset and view failures as learning opportunities. Analyze and learn from failed attempts to refine strategies and improve future decision-making.
- ✓ Celebrate and reward courageous actions: Recognize and reward individuals and teams who demonstrate courage and take bold actions. Celebrate both successful outcomes and the courage to take risks, fostering a culture that values calculated risk-taking.
2. Seizing Opportunities: Eagles seize opportunities when they arise, often displaying quick decision-making and action. They understand the importance of acting promptly to secure their prey and maximize their chances of success. Leaders can learn to seize opportunities by being alert, responsive, and proactive in identifying and capitalizing on favorable circumstances. Example: Mark Zuckerberg, the co-founder and CEO of Facebook, demonstrated boldness by expanding Facebook's services beyond social networking to encompass messaging, virtual reality, and digital payment systems. This enabled Facebook to seize new growth opportunities and diversify its offerings.

Steps for Leaders to Emulate:

- ✓ Develop a keen sense of observation: Be observant and proactive in scanning the business environment for potential opportunities. Stay informed about industry trends, market shifts, and emerging technologies.

- ✓ Foster an entrepreneurial mindset: Encourage an entrepreneurial mindset within the organization, where individuals are encouraged to identify and pursue opportunities. Encourage employees to think creatively and take ownership of their ideas.
- ✓ Encourage cross-functional collaboration: Facilitate collaboration across teams and departments to identify and capitalize on opportunities. Encourage open communication and idea-sharing to maximize collective intelligence and uncover new possibilities.
- ✓ Act promptly and decisively: Train yourself and your team to make prompt and well-informed decisions when opportunities arise. Develop the ability to analyze situations quickly and take action decisively, ensuring that opportunities are not missed.
- ✓ Anticipate future trends and disruptions: Stay ahead of the curve by anticipating future trends, consumer demands, and potential disruptions in the market. Act proactively to position the organization to capitalize on these trends and gain a competitive advantage.
- ✓ Encourage calculated experimentation: Provide resources and support for experimentation and piloting of new ideas. Encourage teams to test and validate new concepts and strategies before scaling up.
- ✓ Foster a culture of innovation: Cultivate a culture that embraces innovation and rewards entrepreneurial thinking. Encourage individuals to challenge the status quo, question assumptions, and explore unconventional ideas.

✓ Learn from successes and failures: Evaluate and learn from both successful opportunities and missed ones. Analyze the factors that contributed to success and identify areas for improvement to capitalize on future opportunities.

By observing how eagles exhibit courage and boldness and applying the corresponding steps, leaders can foster a culture of calculated risk-taking, seize opportunities for growth and innovation, and drive the success of their organizations. By taking calculated risks, acting promptly, and fostering an entrepreneurial mindset, leaders can inspire their teams to embrace boldness and capitalize on opportunities for innovation and growth.

Authenticity and Transparency

Eagles exhibit authenticity in their behavior and display transparency within their social structure. Leaders can learn to be authentic and transparent in their communication, building trust and credibility among their team members.

Eagles exhibit authenticity in their behavior and transparency within their social structure, which contributes to trust and cooperation within their flock. Leaders can learn from eagles' authenticity and transparency and apply it to their leadership practices. Here's a detailed explanation with examples and steps on how eagles exhibit authenticity and transparency, and how leaders can emulate it:

1. Authentic Behavior: Eagles exhibit authentic behavior by being true to their nature and instincts. They do not pretend to be something they are not, and their actions align with their inherent characteristics. This authenticity creates trust and credibility within their flock. Leaders can learn from eagles' authenticity by being genuine and true to themselves, fostering trust and connection with their team members. Example: Howard Schultz, the former CEO of Starbucks, demonstrated authenticity by aligning Starbucks' values with his personal beliefs. He emphasized the importance of social responsibility and sustainability, leading the company to take meaningful actions in these areas.

Steps for Leaders to Emulate:

- ✓ Know and embrace your values: Understand your core values and align your actions and decisions with them. Be clear about what you stand for as a leader and ensure that your behavior reflects these values.
- ✓ Be true to yourself: Embrace your unique qualities and strengths as a leader. Avoid imitating others or trying to fit into a mold that does not resonate with your authentic self. Authenticity comes from being genuine and embracing your own leadership style.
- ✓ Share personal stories and experiences: Share personal stories and experiences that showcase your values and shape your leadership journey. This vulnerability helps establish a genuine connection with your team members and builds trust.
- ✓ Foster open and honest communication: Create an environment that encourages open and honest communication. Encourage team members to express their opinions, concerns, and ideas freely. Be open to feedback and listen actively to understand different perspectives.
- ✓ Admit mistakes and take responsibility: When you make a mistake, acknowledge it openly and take responsibility. Demonstrating humility and accountability reinforces your authenticity and builds trust among team members.
- ✓ Encourage authenticity in others: Create a culture that values authenticity and encourages team members to be true to themselves. Appreciate and recognize individuals who demonstrate authenticity in their actions and interactions.

- ✓ Be consistent in your behavior: Ensure consistency between your words and actions. When your behavior aligns with your values and commitments, it enhances your authenticity and credibility as a leader.
2. Transparency in Communication: Eagles exhibit transparency within their social structure, which fosters cooperation and trust among flock members. They communicate openly, sharing information about their intentions, boundaries, and expectations. Leaders can learn from eagles' transparency by practicing open and transparent communication, promoting trust and alignment within their teams. Example: Elon Musk, the CEO of Tesla and SpaceX, is known for his transparent communication style. He frequently uses social media platforms to provide updates and share insights about his companies' progress and plans, fostering transparency and building trust among stakeholders.

Steps for Leaders to Emulate:
- ✓ Share information openly: Communicate information about the organization's goals, strategies, and challenges openly and transparently. Keep team members informed about important decisions, changes, and updates.
- ✓ Explain the "why" behind decisions: Provide context and rationale behind decisions to help team members understand the reasoning behind them. This clarity increases transparency and reduces ambiguity.

- ✓ Encourage questions and dialogue: Create a culture that encourages open dialogue and questions. Encourage team members to seek clarification and express their concerns or ideas without fear of retribution.
- ✓ Practice active listening: Actively listen to team members' perspectives, concerns, and suggestions. Show genuine interest in their opinions and demonstrate that their input is valued and considered.
- ✓ Share progress and results: Keep team members informed about the progress of projects, initiatives, and goals. Celebrate achievements and share lessons learned from both successes and failures.
- ✓ Be honest about challenges: Acknowledge and address challenges and obstacles openly. Discuss potential risks and uncertainties, and involve the team in finding solutions.
- ✓ Provide constructive feedback: Offer feedback and guidance in a transparent and constructive manner. Be specific, highlighting both strengths and areas for improvement. This transparency helps team members understand their performance and growth areas.
- ✓ Lead by example: Model transparency in your own communication. Share your thought process, reasoning, and emotions when making decisions or facing challenges. This sets the tone for open and transparent communication within the team.

By observing how eagles exhibit authenticity and transparency and applying the corresponding steps, leaders can foster trust, credibility, and alignment within their teams and organizations. By being authentic, embracing transparency, and practicing open communication, leaders can create an environment where team members feel valued, connected, and empowered. This, in turn, enhances collaboration, engagement, and overall team performance.

Strategic Delegation

Eagles delegate responsibilities within their flock, distributing tasks to maximize efficiency. Leaders can learn to delegate strategically, empowering their team members and leveraging their strengths for optimal performance.

Eagles exhibit strategic delegation within their flock, distributing responsibilities to maximize efficiency and effectiveness in their hunting and nesting activities. Leaders can learn from eagles' approach to strategic delegation and apply it to their leadership practices. Here's a detailed explanation with examples and steps on how eagles exhibit strategic delegation and how leaders can emulate it:

1. Distribution of Responsibilities: Eagles distribute responsibilities within their flock based on each individual's strengths and capabilities. They assign tasks such as hunting, nest-building, and caring for the young, ensuring that each member contributes to the overall success of the group. This distribution of responsibilities allows them to optimize their efficiency and increase their chances of survival. Similarly, leaders can learn to strategically delegate tasks to empower their team members and leverage their strengths for optimal performance. Example: In a project management setting, a leader may delegate tasks to team members based on their skills and expertise. Assigning a team member who excels in data analysis to handle the analytical aspects of a project, while assigning a team member with strong

communication skills to manage client interactions.

Steps for Leaders to Emulate:

- ✓ Understand team members' strengths: Take the time to understand the unique strengths, skills, and expertise of each team member. Assess their capabilities and areas of interest to identify suitable tasks for delegation.
- ✓ Match tasks with individual strengths: Assign tasks that align with team members' strengths and interests. Consider their experience, expertise, and potential for growth when determining the appropriate responsibilities to delegate.
- ✓ Provide clear instructions and expectations: Clearly communicate the objectives, expectations, and desired outcomes of the delegated tasks. Ensure that team members have a clear understanding of what needs to be accomplished and any relevant deadlines or constraints.
- ✓ Empower and trust team members: Delegate authority and decision-making power to team members, allowing them to take ownership of their assigned tasks. Trust their abilities and provide the necessary support and resources for successful completion.
- ✓ Establish accountability and milestones: Set clear milestones and checkpoints to track progress and ensure accountability. Regularly review the status of delegated tasks and provide feedback and guidance as needed.
- ✓ Offer support and guidance: Be available to provide guidance, answer questions, and offer support when team members encounter

challenges or need clarification. Provide resources and tools to assist them in accomplishing their delegated tasks effectively.
✓ Encourage collaboration and knowledge sharing: Foster an environment that encourages collaboration and knowledge sharing among team members. Encourage them to seek assistance from one another, share insights, and learn from each other's experiences.
✓ Provide recognition and rewards: Acknowledge and appreciate the contributions of team members who successfully complete delegated tasks. Recognize their efforts and publicly highlight their achievements, reinforcing a culture that values and rewards excellence in performance.
✓ Learn from the delegation process: Reflect on the outcomes of the delegation process. Assess the effectiveness of the assigned tasks, the performance of team members, and the impact on overall productivity and outcomes. Use these insights to refine future delegation strategies.
2. Leveraging Diverse Perspectives: Eagles demonstrate strategic delegation by leveraging the diverse perspectives and abilities of their flock members. Each member contributes their unique strengths and skills, enhancing the overall effectiveness of the group. Leaders can learn from eagles by recognizing the value of diversity within their teams and strategically delegating tasks to capitalize on different perspectives. Example:

In a marketing campaign, a leader may delegate tasks such as content creation, design, data analysis, and customer research to individuals with diverse backgrounds and skill sets. This allows for a holistic and well-rounded approach to the campaign.

Steps for Leaders to Emulate:

- ✓ Embrace diversity: Recognize the value of diverse perspectives, experiences, and skills within your team. Encourage diversity in recruitment and foster an inclusive and respectful work environment.
- ✓ Assess the strengths and expertise of team members: Understand the strengths, expertise, and unique perspectives of team members. Recognize the different skills and backgrounds they bring to the table.
- ✓ Assign tasks strategically: Assign tasks based on individual strengths and areas of expertise. Consider the potential for cross-functional collaboration and the opportunities to leverage diverse perspectives for problem-solving and innovation.
- ✓ Foster collaboration and communication: Encourage collaboration and open communication among team members. Create opportunities for knowledge sharing, brainstorming, and collective decision-making to leverage the diverse perspectives within the team.
- ✓ Facilitate cross-training and learning: Provide opportunities for team members to learn from each other and develop new skills. Encourage cross-training initiatives that allow individuals to expand their knowledge and capabilities.

- ✓ Create a supportive environment: Foster a supportive environment where team members feel comfortable sharing their perspectives and ideas. Encourage respectful and inclusive discussions, ensuring that all voices are heard and valued.
- ✓ Monitor progress and provide feedback: Regularly monitor the progress of delegated tasks and provide feedback to team members. Offer guidance and support to ensure that tasks are completed effectively and aligned with overall objectives.
- ✓ Evaluate outcomes and adjust strategies: Evaluate the outcomes of the delegated tasks and assess the effectiveness of leveraging diverse perspectives. Use the insights gained to adjust delegation strategies and refine future decision-making processes.

By observing how eagles exhibit strategic delegation and applying the corresponding steps, leaders can empower their team members, leverage diverse perspectives, and optimize performance. By understanding team members' strengths, assigning tasks strategically, and fostering collaboration and communication, leaders can drive success, enhance productivity, and promote a culture of shared ownership and growth within their teams and organizations.

Customer-Centricity

Eagles prioritize their hunting efforts to meet their nutritional needs. Leaders can learn to be customer-centric, understanding their customers' needs and delivering exceptional experiences that exceed expectations.

Eagles exhibit a form of customer-centricity in their hunting behavior, prioritizing their efforts to meet their nutritional needs. They focus on understanding their prey, adapting their strategies, and delivering successful outcomes. Leaders can learn from eagles' customer-centric approach and apply it to their leadership practices. Here's a detailed explanation with examples and steps on how eagles exhibit customer-centricity, and how leaders can emulate it:

1. Understanding Customer Needs: Eagles have a deep understanding of their prey and their behaviors. They observe their surroundings, study their prey's patterns, and adapt their hunting strategies accordingly. This understanding allows them to make informed decisions and increase their chances of success. Similarly, leaders can learn to understand their customers' needs by gathering insights, conducting market research, and leveraging data to inform their decision-making. Example: Amazon, the e-commerce giant, demonstrates customer-centricity by continuously gathering data and understanding customer preferences. They analyze customer behavior, purchase history, and feedback to tailor their product offerings, recommendations, and customer experiences.

Steps for Leaders to Emulate:
- ✓ Conduct market research: Invest in market research to understand your target audience, their preferences, pain points, and aspirations. Leverage customer surveys, interviews, and data analysis to gain insights into their needs and expectations.
- ✓ Develop customer personas: Create customer personas that represent different segments of your target audience. Use these personas to develop a deep understanding of their motivations, challenges, and preferences.
- ✓ Listen to customer feedback: Actively seek and listen to customer feedback through various channels, such as surveys, feedback forms, social media, and customer support interactions. Use this feedback to identify areas for improvement and address customer concerns.
- ✓ Analyze customer data: Leverage data analytics to gain insights into customer behavior, preferences, and purchase patterns. Use this data to identify trends, make data-driven decisions, and personalize customer experiences.
- ✓ Anticipate customer needs: Stay ahead of customer needs by anticipating trends, industry shifts, and emerging customer expectations. Proactively adapt your products, services, and experiences to meet evolving customer demands.
- ✓ Foster a customer-centric culture: Instill a customer-centric mindset within your organization. Ensure that all employees, from frontline staff to top-level executives, prioritize

customer satisfaction and understand the importance of meeting customer needs.

- ✓ Empower employees to serve customers: Provide training and resources to empower employees to deliver exceptional customer experiences. Encourage them to go above and beyond to meet customer needs and exceed expectations.
- ✓ Personalize customer experiences: Tailor your products, services, and interactions to meet individual customer preferences. Leverage technology and data to personalize recommendations, offers, and communication.
- ✓ Continuously iterate and improve: Regularly review and iterate your products, services, and processes based on customer feedback and data insights. Continuously seek ways to enhance the customer experience and address changing customer needs.

2. Delivering Exceptional Experiences: Eagles prioritize their hunting efforts to deliver successful outcomes. They demonstrate agility, precision, and adaptability to capture their prey effectively. Similarly, leaders can focus on delivering exceptional experiences that exceed customer expectations. Example: Apple is known for its customer-centric approach, delivering seamless and intuitive products that prioritize user experience. They invest heavily in design, functionality, and customer support to ensure customer satisfaction.

Steps for Leaders to Emulate:

- ✓ Set high standards for customer experience: Establish clear expectations and standards for delivering exceptional customer experiences. Communicate these standards to all employees and hold them accountable for meeting them.

✓ Design with the customer in mind: Incorporate customer feedback and preferences into your product and service design processes. Prioritize usability, functionality, and aesthetics to create experiences that delight and meet customer needs.

✓ Streamline processes and remove friction: Identify and eliminate any barriers or pain points in the customer journey. Streamline processes, reduce complexity, and ensure a seamless and frictionless experience across all touchpoints.

✓ Empower customer-facing teams: Provide training, resources, and decision-making authority to customer-facing teams. Empower them to handle customer inquiries, resolve issues, and deliver personalized experiences.

✓ Practice active listening: Actively listen to customers, showing empathy and understanding. Pay attention to their needs, concerns, and feedback, and take prompt action to address any issues or opportunities for improvement.

✓ Go above and beyond: Encourage employees to go the extra mile to exceed customer expectations. Empower them to surprise and delight customers with unexpected gestures or personalized touches.

✓ Measure customer satisfaction: Implement metrics and feedback mechanisms to measure customer satisfaction. Use customer

satisfaction surveys, Net Promoter Score (NPS), or other indicators to gauge how well you are meeting customer needs.
- ✓ Learn from customer interactions: Continuously learn from customer interactions and feedback. Analyze customer data, track trends, and identify areas for improvement based on customer input.
- ✓ Foster a customer-centric mindset: Cultivate a customer-centric culture within your organization. Ensure that all employees understand the importance of customer satisfaction and are committed to delivering exceptional experiences.

By observing how eagles exhibit customer-centricity and applying the corresponding steps, leaders can foster a culture of understanding, empathy, and exceptional customer experiences. By understanding customer needs, delivering personalized experiences, and continuously improving based on customer feedback, leaders can build long-lasting relationships, loyalty, and advocacy among their customer base.

Global Perspective

Eagles migrate across vast distances, demonstrating a global perspective. Leaders can learn to have a global mindset, embracing diversity and inclusivity, and considering the broader impact of their decisions and actions.

Eagles demonstrate a global perspective through their migratory behavior, traversing vast distances and adapting to different environments. They exhibit a sense of connectedness and understanding of the larger world around them. Leaders can learn from eagles' global perspective and apply it to their leadership practices. Here's a detailed explanation with examples and steps on how eagles exhibit a global perspective, and how leaders can emulate it:

1. Embracing Diversity and Inclusivity: Eagles encounter different environments and interact with various species during their migrations. They adapt to diverse climates, landscapes, and ecosystems. Similarly, leaders can embrace diversity and inclusivity by recognizing and valuing different perspectives, cultures, and backgrounds within their organizations. Example: The multinational company Unilever emphasizes diversity and inclusivity in its leadership practices. They promote gender equality, cultural diversity, and inclusivity through various initiatives and programs.

Steps for Leaders to Emulate:
- ✓ Foster an inclusive culture: Create an inclusive work environment where individuals from different backgrounds feel welcome,

valued, and respected. Embrace diversity in all its forms, including but not limited to race, gender, ethnicity, age, and thought.

✓ Encourage diverse perspectives: Actively seek and encourage diverse perspectives within teams and decision-making processes. Promote open dialogue, listen to diverse viewpoints, and create opportunities for all team members to contribute and be heard.

✓ Build diverse teams: Assemble teams that reflect diverse perspectives, experiences, and skills. Leverage the strengths and unique contributions of individuals from different backgrounds to drive innovation and creativity.

✓ Provide cross-cultural training: Offer cross-cultural training programs to enhance understanding and appreciation of different cultures, customs, and communication styles. This helps foster a global mindset among team members and promotes effective collaboration across borders.

✓ Support employee resource groups: Establish and support employee resource groups that provide a platform for underrepresented groups to connect, share experiences, and drive inclusion. These groups can create awareness, advocate for inclusion, and contribute to organizational initiatives.

✓ Partner with diverse suppliers: Actively seek and partner with diverse suppliers, promoting economic inclusion and empowering local communities. Embrace supplier diversity as part of your procurement strategy, contributing to a more inclusive global supply chain.

- ✓ Provide equal opportunities for growth: Ensure that all employees have equal opportunities for growth, advancement, and recognition. Implement policies and practices that promote diversity and inclusion at all levels of the organization.
- ✓ Celebrate cultural diversity: Organize events and initiatives that celebrate and showcase different cultures, traditions, and perspectives. Encourage team members to share their cultural heritage and promote understanding and appreciation among colleagues.
- ✓ Lead by example: Demonstrate your commitment to diversity and inclusivity through your actions and behaviors. Advocate for fairness, equal opportunities, and respect for all individuals within the organization.
2. Considering the Broader Impact: Eagles' migratory behavior requires them to consider the broader impact of their actions. They adapt their strategies to align with different environments and ecosystems, recognizing the interconnectedness of their actions with the larger ecosystem. Similarly, leaders can develop a global perspective by considering the broader impact of their decisions and actions on a local, regional, and global scale. Example: The Body Shop, a global cosmetics company, incorporates a global perspective into its business practices. They prioritize ethical sourcing, sustainability, and community empowerment, considering the impact of their operations on both people and the planet.

Steps for Leaders to Emulate:

- ✓ Assess the global impact of decisions: Consider the potential local, regional, and global impact of business decisions. Evaluate the environmental, social, and economic consequences of your actions and strive to make choices that benefit both the organization and society.
- ✓ Embrace sustainability practices: Integrate sustainability into business strategies, operations, and products. Aim to minimize the environmental footprint and promote sustainable practices throughout the value chain.
- ✓ Engage in responsible sourcing: Evaluate and select suppliers based on their adherence to ethical and sustainable practices. Consider factors such as fair labor conditions, responsible sourcing of raw materials, and environmental stewardship.
- ✓ Support community and social initiatives: Contribute to the well-being of local and global communities through philanthropic efforts, employee volunteer programs, and partnerships with NGOs. Align your organization's mission and values with initiatives that address social challenges and promote sustainable development.
- ✓ Collaborate with global stakeholders: Establish partnerships and collaborate with organizations, government bodies, and other stakeholders to address global challenges and contribute to positive change. Share knowledge, resources, and expertise to tackle issues that transcend organizational boundaries.

- ✓ Stay informed about global trends: Keep abreast of global trends, geopolitical changes, and emerging technologies that may impact your organization and the wider world. Stay informed about cultural, economic, and technological developments to anticipate and adapt to future changes.
- ✓ Incorporate corporate social responsibility (CSR): Develop and implement a comprehensive CSR strategy that considers environmental, social, and governance aspects. Align your CSR efforts with the United Nations Sustainable Development Goals or other relevant frameworks to address global challenges.
- ✓ Engage employees in global initiatives: Involve employees in global initiatives and projects that promote social responsibility, sustainability, and global citizenship. Encourage their participation and provide opportunities for them to contribute to global causes.
- ✓ Communicate the broader impact: Clearly communicate the broader impact of your organization's actions to employees, stakeholders, and customers. Share success stories, progress, and challenges related to global initiatives to raise awareness and promote transparency.

By observing how eagles exhibit a global perspective and applying the corresponding steps, leaders can embrace diversity and inclusivity, consider the broader impact of their decisions, and foster a global mindset within their organizations. By promoting an inclusive culture, encouraging diverse perspectives, and considering the environmental and social consequences of their actions, leaders can contribute to a more interconnected and sustainable world.

Crisis Management

Eagles exhibit calmness and resilience in the face of adverse conditions or threats. Leaders can learn effective crisis management, staying composed, making decisive decisions, and guiding their teams through challenging times.

Eagles exhibit remarkable crisis management skills, displaying calmness and resilience in the face of adverse conditions or threats. They adapt their strategies, remain composed, and make decisive decisions to navigate through challenging situations. Leaders can learn from eagles' crisis management approach and apply it to their leadership practices. Here's a detailed explanation with examples and steps on how eagles exhibit crisis management skills, and how leaders can emulate them:

1. Composure in Adverse Conditions: Eagles maintain composure and stay focused even in the midst of adverse conditions such as storms or extreme weather. They do not panic or lose their sense of direction. This ability to remain composed is essential for effective crisis management. Example: During the 2008 global financial crisis, Indra Nooyi, the former CEO of PepsiCo, demonstrated composure by taking decisive actions to safeguard the company's financial stability. She implemented cost-cutting measures, streamlined operations, and focused on innovation to navigate through the crisis successfully.

Steps for Leaders to Emulate:

- ✓ Stay calm and composed: As a leader, it's crucial to maintain composure during a crisis. Stay focused, keep emotions in check, and project a sense of stability and confidence to inspire your team.
- ✓ Assess the situation: Gather accurate and timely information about the crisis to understand its scope, impact, and potential risks. Analyze the available data and consult relevant stakeholders to make informed decisions.
- ✓ Communicate transparently: Keep your team members and stakeholders informed about the crisis and its implications. Communicate with transparency, providing regular updates and addressing concerns to build trust and alleviate anxiety.
- ✓ Evaluate risks and potential consequences: Assess the risks associated with the crisis and identify potential consequences for your organization. Consider the short-term and long-term impacts and develop contingency plans to mitigate risks.
- ✓ Anticipate challenges and plan accordingly: Anticipate potential challenges that may arise during the crisis and develop strategies to address them proactively. Identify potential obstacles, resources required, and steps needed to overcome them.
- ✓ Prioritize and make decisive decisions: Identify the most critical issues and prioritize actions based on their potential impact and urgency. Make decisive decisions, taking into account the available information, risks, and desired outcomes.

- ✓ Empower your team: Delegate responsibilities and empower your team members to act within their areas of expertise. Provide clear guidelines, resources, and support to enable them to contribute effectively to crisis management efforts.
- ✓ Foster collaboration and teamwork: Encourage collaboration and teamwork during a crisis. Create cross-functional teams, establish clear lines of communication, and promote the sharing of ideas and knowledge to leverage collective intelligence.
- ✓ Monitor and adapt: Continuously monitor the progress of crisis management efforts and adjust strategies as needed. Stay flexible and open to making changes based on emerging information or shifting circumstances.
- ✓ Learn from the crisis: Once the crisis has passed, conduct a thorough review and analysis of the crisis management process. Identify lessons learned, areas for improvement, and implement changes to enhance future crisis preparedness.

2. Decisiveness and Rapid Action: Eagles demonstrate decisiveness and take swift action when faced with threats or challenging situations. They adapt their strategies, make quick decisions, and execute them effectively. This ability to act rapidly is crucial for effective crisis management. Example: During the Deepwater Horizon oil spill crisis in 2010, Bob Dudley, the then-CEO of BP, demonstrated decisiveness by taking immediate action to stop the spill, coordinate cleanup efforts, and

communicate transparently with stakeholders to mitigate the impact.

Steps for Leaders to Emulate:

- ✓ Gather relevant information: Gather accurate and relevant information about the crisis to make informed decisions. Consult subject matter experts, seek input from key stakeholders, and analyze data to gain a comprehensive understanding of the situation.
- ✓ Define clear objectives: Clearly define the objectives to be achieved during the crisis. Establish specific, measurable, achievable, relevant, and time-bound (SMART) goals to guide decision-making and action.
- ✓ Develop contingency plans: Anticipate potential scenarios and develop contingency plans to address each situation. Consider different courses of action, assess their potential outcomes, and determine the most effective response strategy.
- ✓ Establish a crisis management team: Assemble a dedicated crisis management team comprising key leaders and subject matter experts. Assign roles and responsibilities, establish clear lines of communication, and ensure that team members are empowered to make decisions within their areas of expertise.
- ✓ Delegate authority and empower decision-making: Delegate authority to the crisis management team members, empowering them to make rapid decisions and take appropriate actions. Establish a framework for decision-making and provide guidelines to

ensure alignment with the organization's values and objectives.

✓ Communicate effectively: Develop a robust communication plan to keep all stakeholders informed about the crisis, its impact, and the actions being taken. Ensure clear and timely communication, addressing concerns, and providing regular updates to instill confidence and manage expectations.

✓ Mobilize resources: Identify and allocate the necessary resources to support crisis management efforts. This includes financial resources, personnel, equipment, and any external support required to effectively address the crisis.

✓ Monitor progress and adjust strategies: Continuously monitor the progress of crisis management activities. Regularly evaluate the effectiveness of implemented strategies, adjust plans as needed, and ensure that actions align with the evolving situation.

✓ Learn and improve: Once the crisis is resolved, conduct a thorough review of the crisis management process. Identify areas of strength and areas for improvement, document lessons learned, and update crisis management protocols and strategies accordingly.

By observing how eagles exhibit crisis management skills and applying the corresponding steps, leaders can effectively navigate through challenging times. By maintaining composure, making decisive decisions, empowering their teams, and adapting strategies, leaders can lead their organizations through crises with resilience and success.

Strategic Innovation

Eagles exhibit innovative hunting techniques, adapting their strategies to changing circumstances. Leaders can learn to drive strategic innovation within their organizations, encouraging creativity and exploring new opportunities for growth.

Eagles exhibit strategic innovation in their hunting techniques, adapting their strategies to changing circumstances and exploring new opportunities for success. They demonstrate creativity, agility, and a willingness to try new approaches. Leaders can learn from eagles' strategic innovation and apply it to their leadership practices. Here's a detailed explanation with examples and steps on how eagles exhibit strategic innovation, and how leaders can emulate them:

1. Adapting to Changing Circumstances: Eagles face various challenges and changing circumstances in their hunting environment. They adapt their strategies based on factors such as weather conditions, prey availability, and competition. This adaptability allows them to maximize their hunting success. Similarly, leaders can foster a culture of adaptability and agility within their organizations. Example: Netflix, the streaming service provider, demonstrated strategic innovation by adapting to changing consumer behavior and technological advancements. They shifted their business model from DVD rentals to online streaming, disrupting the traditional media industry.

Steps for Leaders to Emulate:

- ✓ Foster a culture of innovation: Create an organizational culture that values and encourages innovation. Promote an environment where employees feel empowered to share new ideas, experiment with new approaches, and challenge the status quo.
- ✓ Encourage creativity and divergent thinking: Provide opportunities for employees to think creatively and generate innovative solutions. Encourage brainstorming sessions, cross-functional collaboration, and the exploration of diverse perspectives to foster a culture of creativity and innovation.
- ✓ Embrace a growth mindset: Cultivate a growth mindset within the organization, where failure is seen as a learning opportunity and experimentation is encouraged. Encourage employees to take calculated risks and learn from both successes and failures.
- ✓ Invest in research and development: Allocate resources to research and development initiatives to explore new technologies, trends, and market opportunities. Encourage teams to experiment and prototype new ideas, products, or services.
- ✓ Stay informed about industry trends: Continuously monitor and analyze industry trends, technological advancements, and changing customer preferences. Stay ahead of the curve by understanding emerging opportunities and potential disruptions.
- ✓ Empower innovation champions: Identify and empower individuals who are passionate about innovation and strategic thinking.

Encourage them to spearhead innovation initiatives, lead cross-functional teams, and drive change within the organization.

✓ Create cross-functional collaboration: Foster collaboration and knowledge-sharing across different departments and teams. Break down silos to encourage diverse perspectives and cross-pollination of ideas, leading to innovative solutions.

✓ Provide resources and support: Ensure that employees have access to the necessary resources, tools, and training to support their innovative efforts. Create dedicated innovation spaces, allocate budgets for experimentation, and provide training in design thinking or other innovation methodologies.

✓ Celebrate and reward innovation: Recognize and celebrate innovative ideas and successful implementation. Establish reward and recognition programs that acknowledge and encourage employees' contributions to innovation.

✓ Develop strategic partnerships: Collaborate with external partners, such as startups, research institutions, or industry experts, to tap into external expertise, access new technologies, and explore innovative opportunities.

2. Exploring New Opportunities: Eagles are constantly on the lookout for new hunting opportunities. They scan their surroundings, identify potential prey, and explore different hunting grounds. Similarly, leaders can encourage their teams to explore new opportunities for growth and innovation.

Example: Google, the multinational technology company, exemplifies strategic innovation by constantly exploring new areas beyond its core search engine business. They have diversified into various domains such as cloud computing, artificial intelligence, and autonomous vehicles.

Steps for Leaders to Emulate:

✓ Encourage curiosity and exploration: Foster a culture of curiosity and encourage employees to explore new ideas, markets, and technologies. Provide opportunities for learning, cross-functional exposure, and collaboration to fuel innovation and uncover new opportunities.

✓ Conduct market research: Invest in market research to identify emerging trends, customer needs, and potential gaps in the market. Use data-driven insights to identify new market segments or areas where the organization can differentiate itself.

✓ Foster cross-pollination of ideas: Encourage employees to look beyond their immediate responsibilities and engage with different departments or teams. Encourage knowledge-sharing, brainstorming sessions, and collaboration across diverse functions to generate innovative ideas and discover new opportunities.

✓ Encourage calculated risk-taking: Foster a culture that supports calculated risk-taking. Encourage employees to propose and test new ideas, providing them with the necessary support and resources to experiment and learn from the outcomes.

- ✓ Create a dedicated innovation team: Establish a dedicated team or department focused on driving innovation within the organization. Empower them to explore new opportunities, conduct experiments, and identify potential growth areas.
- ✓ Seek customer feedback and insights: Regularly seek feedback from customers to understand their evolving needs and preferences. Engage in customer co-creation or feedback sessions to gain insights that can drive innovative product or service offerings.
- ✓ Monitor industry disruptions and emerging technologies: Keep a close eye on industry disruptions and emerging technologies that have the potential to impact your business. Stay informed about new market entrants, startups, or disruptive business models that may present opportunities or threats.
- ✓ Develop a process for idea evaluation and implementation: Establish a structured process for evaluating and prioritizing new ideas or opportunities. Define criteria for assessing their feasibility, market potential, and alignment with the organization's strategic goals. Develop a framework for implementing and scaling selected ideas.
- ✓ Encourage external partnerships and collaborations: Seek external partnerships or collaborations with startups, universities, or industry experts to gain access to cutting-edge technologies, research, or market insights. Leverage their expertise to identify and explore new opportunities.

By observing how eagles exhibit strategic innovation and applying the corresponding steps, leaders can foster a culture of innovation, adapt to changing circumstances, and explore new opportunities for growth. By encouraging creativity, embracing agility, and exploring diverse avenues, leaders can drive strategic innovation within their organizations and stay ahead in an ever-evolving business landscape.

Data-Driven Decision Making

Eagles rely on their keen eyesight and observations to make informed decisions in their hunting activities. Leaders can learn to leverage data and analytics to make evidence-based decisions, ensuring accuracy and effectiveness in their strategies.

Eagles rely on their keen eyesight and observations to make informed decisions during their hunting activities. Similarly, leaders can adopt a data-driven decision-making approach, leveraging data and analytics to make evidence-based decisions. This approach ensures accuracy, effectiveness, and improved outcomes in their strategies. Here's a detailed explanation with examples and steps on how eagles exhibit data-driven decision making, and how leaders can emulate them:

1. Gathering and Analyzing Data: Eagles rely on their sharp eyesight and keen observation skills to gather data about their prey, such as their behavior, location, and movements. This data provides crucial insights for making informed decisions during the hunting process. Leaders can emulate this by gathering relevant data and analyzing it to gain insights into their business operations, market trends, customer preferences, and other key factors. Example: Amazon, the global e-commerce giant, exemplifies data-driven decision making by collecting and analyzing vast amounts of customer data. They use this data to personalize recommendations, optimize supply chain

operations, and make strategic business decisions.

Steps for Leaders to Emulate:
- ✓ Identify key data sources: Determine the relevant data sources within your organization, such as customer data, sales data, operational data, market research, and external sources. Identify the data points that are critical for decision making.
- ✓ Establish data collection mechanisms: Implement systems and processes to collect data efficiently and accurately. Leverage technology tools, such as customer relationship management (CRM) systems, data analytics platforms, and surveys, to gather data from various sources.
- ✓ Clean and validate data: Ensure the quality and accuracy of the collected data by cleaning and validating it. Eliminate duplicate or irrelevant data, correct any errors or inconsistencies, and ensure data integrity.
- ✓ Analyze and interpret data: Utilize data analytics tools and techniques to analyze and interpret the collected data. Apply statistical methods, data visualization techniques, and predictive analytics to gain insights and identify patterns, trends, or correlations.
- ✓ Apply data-driven frameworks: Adopt data-driven frameworks or methodologies, such as the "SMART" framework (Specific, Measurable, Achievable, Relevant, Time-bound), to guide decision making. Use data to set goals, track progress, and evaluate outcomes.

- ✓ Make evidence-based decisions: Use the insights derived from data analysis to make evidence-based decisions. Combine quantitative data with qualitative insights and expertise to ensure a comprehensive understanding of the situation.
- ✓ Foster a data-driven culture: Instill a data-driven culture within the organization by promoting the use of data in decision making at all levels. Encourage employees to base their arguments and recommendations on data, and provide training and resources to enhance data literacy.
- ✓ Continuously update and refine data analysis processes: Regularly evaluate and refine data analysis processes to improve accuracy, efficiency, and relevance. Stay updated with advancements in data analytics technologies and methodologies to leverage the full potential of data.
- ✓ Monitor and measure outcomes: Establish metrics and key performance indicators (KPIs) to monitor the outcomes of data-driven decisions. Continuously evaluate the impact of decisions, track progress, and make adjustments as needed based on ongoing data analysis.

2. Leveraging Predictive Analytics: Eagles rely on their observations and instincts to predict the behavior and movements of their prey. Similarly, leaders can leverage predictive analytics techniques to forecast future trends, customer behavior, and market dynamics. This enables them to make proactive and informed decisions. Example: Netflix uses

predictive analytics to recommend personalized content to its users. By analyzing user viewing patterns, preferences, and historical data, they can predict the type of content that users are likely to enjoy, increasing customer satisfaction and retention.

Steps for Leaders to Emulate:

- ✓ Identify relevant predictive variables: Determine the key variables or factors that can predict future outcomes or behaviors within your business context. These may include customer demographics, purchase history, website interactions, or market indicators.
- ✓ Gather historical data: Collect historical data related to the identified predictive variables. Ensure that the data is comprehensive, accurate, and representative of the time period and population of interest.
- ✓ Utilize predictive analytics tools and techniques: Leverage predictive analytics tools and techniques, such as machine learning algorithms, regression analysis, or time series forecasting, to analyze the historical data and generate predictions or forecasts.
- ✓ Validate and refine predictive models: Validate the accuracy and reliability of the predictive models by comparing their predictions with actual outcomes. Continuously refine and improve the models based on feedback and new data to enhance their predictive power.
- ✓ Incorporate predictive insights into decision making: Integrate the predictive insights into the decision-making process. Consider the

predictions as valuable inputs when formulating strategies, setting goals, allocating resources, or making product/service-related decisions.
✓ Test and learn: Implement pilot projects or A/B tests based on the predictive insights to validate their effectiveness and impact. Monitor the outcomes and make adjustments based on the results to optimize the use of predictive analytics in decision making.
✓ Continuously update models: Regularly update the predictive models to incorporate new data and ensure their relevance and accuracy. Monitor changes in the business environment and customer behavior to adapt the models accordingly.
✓ Develop a culture of experimentation: Encourage experimentation and a test-and-learn approach to refine predictive models and enhance their accuracy. Embrace failure as an opportunity for learning and improvement.
✓ Seek expert guidance if needed: If you lack in-house expertise in predictive analytics, consider partnering with data scientists or analytics consultants who can provide guidance and support in implementing and refining predictive models.

By observing how eagles exhibit data-driven decision making and applying the corresponding steps, leaders can harness the power of data and analytics to make informed decisions. By gathering and analyzing data, leveraging predictive analytics, and fostering a data-driven culture, leaders can enhance the accuracy and effectiveness of their strategies, leading to improved outcomes and business success.

Mentorship and Development

Eagles mentor and guide their young, teaching them essential hunting skills. Leaders can learn to be mentors and coaches, supporting the development and growth of their team members, unlocking their full potential.

Eagles exhibit mentorship and development by guiding and teaching their young how to hunt and survive in their natural habitat. They provide valuable guidance, support, and training to help their offspring develop essential skills. Similarly, leaders can adopt a mentorship and development approach, supporting the growth and potential of their team members. Here's a detailed explanation with examples and steps on how eagles exhibit mentorship and development, and how leaders can emulate them:

1. Guiding and Sharing Knowledge: Eagles play a crucial role in guiding and sharing knowledge with their young. They teach them essential hunting skills, including flight techniques, hunting strategies, and how to navigate their environment. Similarly, leaders can guide and share their knowledge and expertise to support the development of their team members. Example: Satya Nadella, the CEO of Microsoft, is known for his mentorship approach. He regularly conducts "skip-level" meetings, where he meets with employees at different levels of the organization, providing guidance and insights to support their growth and development.

Steps for Leaders to Emulate:

- ✓ Establish a mentorship mindset: Recognize the importance of mentorship and embrace a mindset of supporting and developing others. Value the growth and potential of your team members and commit to their professional development.
- ✓ Foster a learning culture: Create an environment that values continuous learning and development. Encourage employees to seek learning opportunities, provide access to training and resources, and celebrate and recognize individual growth and achievements.
- ✓ Identify mentees and their development needs: Identify team members who would benefit from mentorship and support. Understand their strengths, weaknesses, and development goals. Engage in open and honest conversations to identify areas where they require guidance and support.
- ✓ Provide constructive feedback: Offer regular and constructive feedback to help mentees understand their strengths and areas for improvement. Provide specific and actionable suggestions for growth, and create a safe and supportive environment where individuals feel comfortable receiving feedback.
- ✓ Share personal experiences and insights: Share your own experiences and lessons learned throughout your career. Provide real-life examples of challenges faced and how you overcame them. Use these stories to inspire and guide your mentees, helping them navigate their own professional journeys.

- ✓ Offer guidance and resources: Provide guidance on professional development opportunities, such as training programs, certifications, or conferences. Share relevant articles, books, or podcasts that can enhance their knowledge and skills.
- ✓ Set development goals: Collaborate with mentees to set clear and achievable development goals. Break down these goals into actionable steps and help them create a roadmap for success. Regularly review progress, provide guidance, and adjust goals as needed.
- ✓ Encourage networking and exposure: Encourage mentees to expand their professional network and gain exposure to different aspects of the business. Facilitate introductions, provide opportunities for cross-functional collaboration, and support their involvement in industry events or professional associations.
- ✓ Act as a role model: Lead by example and demonstrate the qualities and behaviors you expect from your mentees. Model effective communication, ethical decision-making, and continuous learning. Display a commitment to personal and professional growth.
- ✓ Create opportunities for stretch assignments: Provide opportunities for mentees to take on challenging projects or assignments that stretch their skills and capabilities. Offer guidance and support as they navigate these opportunities, helping them build confidence and competence.

✓ Celebrate milestones and successes: Recognize and celebrate the milestones and achievements of your mentees. Acknowledge their growth, effort, and dedication. This fosters a sense of accomplishment and motivation to continue their development journey.

2. Encouraging Autonomy and Empowerment: Eagles gradually allow their young to practice their hunting skills, encouraging autonomy and independence. They provide opportunities for them to develop their abilities while still offering guidance and support. Similarly, leaders can empower their team members to take ownership of their work and make independent decisions. Example: Sheryl Sandberg, the COO of Facebook, emphasizes empowering and developing her team members. She encourages them to take risks, make decisions, and learn from their experiences, fostering a culture of autonomy and growth.

Steps for Leaders to Emulate:

✓ Delegate responsibilities: Assign meaningful tasks and projects to your team members, allowing them to take ownership and develop their skills. Provide clear guidelines and expectations, but also give them the freedom to approach the work in their own way.

✓ Encourage independent thinking: Foster a culture that values independent thinking and encourages individuals to bring their unique perspectives to problem-solving. Encourage team members to think critically, challenge assumptions, and propose innovative solutions.

- ✓ Provide guidance and support: Be available to provide guidance and support when needed. Offer advice, brainstorm ideas together, and help mentees navigate challenges. Balance providing assistance with allowing them to find their own solutions.
- ✓ Encourage risk-taking: Create an environment where calculated risks are encouraged and failure is seen as a learning opportunity. Encourage team members to step out of their comfort zones, try new approaches, and learn from both successes and setbacks.
- ✓ Offer autonomy with accountability: Provide autonomy for decision-making and problem-solving, but also establish accountability measures. Set clear expectations, define performance indicators, and establish regular check-ins to track progress and provide feedback.
- ✓ Foster a supportive network: Encourage the development of peer networks or communities where team members can share knowledge, seek advice, and learn from one another. Facilitate mentorship opportunities beyond your own guidance, allowing mentees to benefit from diverse perspectives.
- ✓ Celebrate growth and independence: Acknowledge and celebrate the growth and independent achievements of your team members. Recognize their ability to take ownership and make decisions. Share success stories to inspire and motivate others.

✓ Continuously provide learning opportunities: Offer ongoing learning and development opportunities to support the growth of your team members. Provide access to training, mentorship programs, workshops, or conferences that enhance their skills and knowledge.
✓ Be open to reverse mentoring: Embrace the opportunity to learn from your mentees. Be open to receiving feedback, insights, and ideas from them. This not only empowers mentees but also demonstrates that learning is a two-way process.

By observing how eagles exhibit mentorship and development and applying the corresponding steps, leaders can create a supportive and growth-oriented environment. By guiding, supporting, and empowering their team members, leaders can foster professional growth, unlock potential, and cultivate a culture of continuous development within their organizations.

Work-Life Balance

Eagles maintain a balance between their hunting activities and other aspects of their lives. Leaders can learn to prioritize work-life balance, setting an example for their teams and promoting the well-being and mental health of their employees.

Eagles exhibit a natural sense of work-life balance by effectively managing their hunting activities while maintaining other aspects of their lives, such as nesting, caring for their young, and rest. Similarly, leaders can learn to prioritize work-life balance, setting an example for their teams and promoting the well-being and mental health of their employees. Here's a detailed explanation with examples and steps on how eagles exhibit work-life balance, and how leaders can emulate them:

1. Prioritizing Essential Activities: Eagles prioritize their hunting activities as a means of survival while also dedicating time to nesting, caring for their young, and rest. Similarly, leaders can prioritize essential activities and set boundaries to ensure a healthy work-life balance for themselves and their teams. Example: Arianna Huffington, co-founder of The Huffington Post, emphasizes the importance of work-life balance and self-care. She promotes practices such as getting enough sleep, taking breaks, and unplugging from technology to enhance well-being and productivity.

Steps for Leaders to Emulate:

✓ Reflect on personal work-life balance: Assess your own work-life balance and identify areas where improvements can be made. Reflect on the impact that your current balance has on your well-being, productivity, and overall satisfaction.

✓ Set clear boundaries: Establish clear boundaries between work and personal life. Define specific times for work-related activities and dedicate time for personal and family activities. Communicate these boundaries to your team members and encourage them to do the same.

✓ Encourage time off and vacation: Encourage your team members to take time off and utilize their vacation days. Foster a culture that values and supports time away from work, allowing employees to recharge and rejuvenate.

✓ Lead by example: Model healthy work-life balance by demonstrating it in your own behavior. Avoid overworking, take breaks when needed, and utilize your time off. Share your experiences and the benefits of work-life balance with your team.

✓ Promote flexible work arrangements: Offer flexible work arrangements such as remote work, flexible hours, or compressed workweeks. Provide opportunities for employees to balance their personal obligations and work responsibilities effectively.

✓ Encourage self-care: Promote self-care practices among your team members. Encourage regular exercise, adequate sleep, and stress-management techniques. Provide resources or wellness programs that support employee well-being.

✓ Minimize after-hours work expectations: Be mindful of after-hours communication and minimize the expectation of immediate responses outside regular work hours. Encourage a healthy separation between work and personal life.

✓ Support workload management: Help your team members effectively manage their workloads. Encourage open communication about work demands, provide resources and support when necessary, and help prioritize tasks to prevent burnout.

✓ Foster a supportive culture: Create a culture that values work-life balance and supports employee well-being. Encourage open conversations about work-life balance, promote empathy and understanding among team members, and provide support for those facing personal challenges.

✓ Regularly assess work-life balance: Continuously monitor and assess work-life balance within your team. Solicit feedback from team members, conduct surveys, or hold regular check-ins to identify areas for improvement and implement necessary adjustments.

2. Promoting Well-being and Mental Health: Eagles prioritize their physical and mental well-being, as it directly affects their hunting abilities and overall survival. Similarly, leaders can prioritize employee well-being and mental health, creating a supportive and healthy work environment. Example: Deloitte, a global

professional services firm, emphasizes employee well-being by offering resources such as mental health programs, work-life balance initiatives, and flexibility options. They understand that employee well-being contributes to productivity and organizational success.

Steps for Leaders to Emulate:

- ✓ Foster an open and supportive culture: Create a work environment where employees feel safe to discuss mental health concerns and seek support. Promote a culture of compassion, understanding, and empathy among team members.
- ✓ Provide mental health resources: Offer access to mental health resources, such as employee assistance programs (EAP), counseling services, or workshops on stress management and resilience. Ensure employees are aware of and encouraged to utilize these resources.
- ✓ Encourage breaks and self-care: Encourage employees to take regular breaks throughout the day, allowing them time for relaxation, rejuvenation, and self-care activities. Promote the importance of physical exercise, mindfulness practices, and stress-reduction techniques.
- ✓ Support work-life integration: Recognize that work and personal life often intertwine. Support employees in integrating their work responsibilities with their personal obligations, allowing for flexibility when needed.
- ✓ Address work overload and burnout: Be attentive to signs of work overload and burnout among team members. Encourage

open communication, provide support, and proactively address workload issues to prevent burnout.

✓ Promote work-life balance initiatives: Implement initiatives that support work-life balance, such as flexible work hours, remote work options, or wellness programs. Communicate and actively promote these initiatives to ensure employee awareness and participation.

✓ Lead with empathy: Practice active listening and empathy when engaging with team members. Be responsive and understanding of their personal challenges, allowing for accommodations or adjustments when needed.

✓ Educate on stress management: Provide education and resources on stress management, resilience, and mindfulness. Conduct workshops or invite guest speakers to address topics related to mental health and well-being.

✓ Celebrate achievements and milestones: Recognize and celebrate individual and team achievements, acknowledging the value of their contributions and efforts. Create opportunities for socialization and team-building activities to foster a positive work environment.

✓ Seek feedback and continuously improve: Regularly seek feedback from employees regarding work-life balance initiatives and mental health support. Use their input to identify areas for improvement and implement changes accordingly.

By observing how eagles exhibit work-life balance and applying the corresponding steps, leaders can create a supportive and healthy work environment that prioritizes employee well-being. By setting an example, promoting work-life balance initiatives, and fostering a culture of well-being, leaders can enhance employee satisfaction, productivity, and overall organizational success.

Social Responsibility

Eagles contribute to their ecosystem by maintaining a balance in the food chain. Leaders can learn to prioritize social responsibility, considering the impact of their decisions on various stakeholders and actively contributing to the betterment of society.

Eagles exhibit social responsibility by playing a vital role in maintaining the balance of their ecosystem as apex predators. They contribute to the food chain by controlling populations of prey species and preventing overpopulation. Similarly, leaders can prioritize social responsibility by considering the impact of their decisions on various stakeholders, including employees, customers, communities, and the environment. Here's a detailed explanation with examples and steps on how eagles exhibit social responsibility, and how leaders can emulate them:

1. Stakeholder Consideration: Eagles indirectly benefit various stakeholders within their ecosystem by helping to maintain a balanced food chain. They contribute to the well-being of other animal populations, including prey species, by preventing overpopulation. Similarly, leaders can prioritize stakeholder consideration by assessing the impact of their decisions on employees, customers, communities, and the environment. Example: Patagonia, an outdoor clothing and gear company, is known for its commitment to social and environmental responsibility. They prioritize sustainability, fair labor practices, and community engagement, considering the

impact of their business decisions on various stakeholders.

Steps for Leaders to Emulate:

✓ Identify key stakeholders: Identify the key stakeholders that are impacted by your organization's activities. This may include employees, customers, local communities, suppliers, shareholders, and the environment.

✓ Assess impacts and risks: Analyze the potential impacts and risks associated with your organization's decisions and actions. Consider social, environmental, and economic factors. Assess the potential positive and negative consequences for different stakeholder groups.

✓ Integrate social responsibility into decision making: Incorporate social responsibility considerations into your decision-making processes. Evaluate options based on their alignment with ethical principles, sustainability goals, and the well-being of stakeholders.

✓ Engage with stakeholders: Foster open dialogue and engagement with stakeholders. Seek their perspectives, input, and feedback on matters that affect them. This can be done through surveys, focus groups, town hall meetings, or ongoing communication channels.

✓ Establish ethical guidelines and policies: Develop and communicate ethical guidelines and policies that outline your organization's commitment to social responsibility. Clearly define expectations and standards of conduct for employees, suppliers, and partners.

- ✓ Support employee well-being: Prioritize the well-being and growth of your employees. Offer fair wages, benefits, and opportunities for professional development. Create a supportive and inclusive work environment that values diversity and work-life balance.
- ✓ Embrace sustainability practices: Integrate sustainability practices into your organization's operations and supply chain. Reduce environmental impacts, promote resource efficiency, and seek eco-friendly alternatives. Engage in responsible sourcing and minimize waste generation.
- ✓ Foster community engagement: Support and contribute to the communities in which your organization operates. Identify opportunities for community involvement, such as volunteering, partnerships with local organizations, or philanthropic initiatives aligned with your mission and values.
- ✓ Transparency and accountability: Communicate your organization's social responsibility efforts transparently. Share progress, achievements, and challenges with stakeholders. Regularly report on your sustainability initiatives, ethical practices, and community contributions.
- ✓ Continual improvement: Embrace a mindset of continual improvement in social responsibility. Regularly evaluate and reassess your organization's impact on stakeholders and the environment. Seek feedback, adapt strategies, and set goals for ongoing improvement.

Environmental Stewardship: Eagles indirectly contribute to environmental stewardship by playing a role in maintaining a balanced ecosystem. Their presence helps regulate populations of prey species, preventing overgrazing and promoting biodiversity. Similarly, leaders can prioritize environmental stewardship by considering the environmental impact of their operations and actively working towards sustainability. Example: Interface, a global modular flooring company, is committed to sustainability and environmental stewardship. They aim to have a net-positive impact on the environment by reducing their carbon footprint, promoting renewable energy, and implementing closed-loop manufacturing processes.

Steps for Leaders to Emulate:

- ✓ Conduct environmental impact assessments: Assess the environmental impact of your organization's activities across the entire value chain. Consider factors such as energy consumption, greenhouse gas emissions, waste generation, water usage, and resource depletion.
- ✓ Set sustainability goals: Establish clear and measurable sustainability goals that align with your organization's mission and values. These goals may include reducing carbon emissions, adopting renewable energy sources, minimizing waste, or promoting recycling initiatives.
- ✓ Implement eco-friendly practices: Integrate environmentally friendly practices into your operations. This can include energy-efficient technologies, waste reduction strategies, water conservation measures, and responsible sourcing of raw materials.
- ✓ Engage suppliers and partners: Collaborate with suppliers and partners to promote

sustainable practices throughout the supply chain. Encourage responsible sourcing, fair labor practices, and environmental compliance.

✓ Promote employee awareness and involvement: Educate and engage employees in environmental sustainability initiatives. Encourage behaviors such as recycling, energy conservation, and responsible resource usage. Provide training on sustainability practices and encourage employee suggestions for improvement.

✓ Invest in innovation and research: Allocate resources to research and development efforts that focus on sustainable technologies and practices. Encourage innovation within your organization to find creative solutions for environmental challenges.

✓ Advocate for environmental protection: Actively participate in initiatives that promote environmental protection and sustainability. Support industry-wide efforts, collaborate with environmental organizations, and engage in public advocacy for responsible environmental policies.

✓ Monitor and report on environmental performance: Regularly monitor and measure your organization's environmental performance. Report on progress, achievements, and challenges to stakeholders. Use these reports as a tool for accountability and as a basis for continual improvement.

- ✓ Certifications and standards: Pursue certifications and adhere to internationally recognized

Humility and Continuous Learning

Eagles display humility in their interactions with their flock, recognizing their role within the social structure. Leaders can learn to practice humility and embrace a mindset of continuous learning, recognizing that there is always room for improvement and seeking knowledge from others.

Eagles exhibit humility in their interactions within their flock, recognizing their role within the social structure and valuing the contributions of other eagles. They display a continuous learning mindset by observing and adapting to their environment, incorporating new hunting techniques, and sharing knowledge within their flock. Similarly, leaders can practice humility and embrace a mindset of continuous learning, acknowledging that they can always improve and seeking knowledge and insights from others. Here's a detailed explanation with examples and steps on how eagles exhibit humility and continuous learning, and how leaders can emulate them:

1. Acknowledging and Valuing Contributions: Eagles demonstrate humility by acknowledging the contributions of other eagles within their flock. They understand that each member has a role to play and respects the expertise and strengths of others. Leaders can emulate this by acknowledging and valuing the contributions of their team members and fostering a culture of appreciation. Example: Warren Buffett, one of the most successful investors, is known for his humility and recognition of others' contributions. He frequently acknowledges

and credits the efforts of his team members, highlighting their contributions to his investment success.

Steps for Leaders to Emulate:

✓ Foster a culture of appreciation: Create an environment where team members feel valued and appreciated. Recognize and acknowledge individual and team achievements. Celebrate successes and publicly express gratitude for the contributions of others.

✓ Encourage diverse perspectives: Embrace diverse perspectives and encourage team members to share their ideas and opinions. Create opportunities for open dialogue and collaboration, fostering an inclusive environment where everyone's input is respected and considered.

✓ Actively listen: Practice active listening by genuinely paying attention to what others have to say. Be present in conversations, ask for clarification, and demonstrate empathy. Make it a habit to listen more and speak less, allowing space for others to share their thoughts and perspectives.

✓ Seek feedback: Actively seek feedback from team members, peers, and stakeholders. Be open to constructive criticism and view it as an opportunity for growth. Embrace feedback as a tool to improve yourself and your leadership approach.

✓ Share credit and success: Share credit and success with your team members. Acknowledge the collective effort that goes into achieving goals and give credit where it is due. Publicly recognize the contributions of individuals and teams in team meetings, presentations, or organizational communications.

✓ Promote collaboration and teamwork: Encourage collaboration and teamwork within your organization. Foster an environment where individuals feel comfortable working together and supporting one another's success. Emphasize the collective achievement rather than individual recognition.

✓ Be approachable and accessible: Maintain an approachable demeanor and an open-door policy. Make yourself available to listen to the ideas and concerns of your team members. Create opportunities for informal interactions where individuals feel comfortable approaching you with questions or suggestions.

✓ Model humility: Lead by example and demonstrate humility in your own behavior. Be willing to admit mistakes and take responsibility for them. Show vulnerability and a willingness to learn from others, inspiring your team members to do the same.

✓ Embrace a growth mindset: Cultivate a growth mindset within yourself and your team. Encourage a belief that abilities and skills can be developed through dedication and hard work. Emphasize the importance of continuous learning and improvement.

✓ Encourage peer learning: Facilitate opportunities for peer learning and knowledge sharing within your organization. Encourage employees to share their expertise and learn from one another. Foster a culture where individuals are comfortable seeking advice and guidance from their peers.

2. Embracing a Mindset of Continuous Learning: Eagles exhibit a mindset of continuous learning by observing their environment, adapting their hunting techniques, and sharing knowledge within their flock. They are open to learning from their experiences and are constantly seeking new ways to improve. Leaders can emulate this mindset by embracing a culture of continuous learning and personal development. Example: Satya Nadella, the CEO of Microsoft, is known for his focus on continuous learning and growth. He encourages his employees to embrace a growth mindset and invest in their own development.

Steps for Leaders to Emulate:

- ✓ Foster a learning culture: Create an environment that values continuous learning and development. Encourage employees to seek learning opportunities, provide access to training and resources, and celebrate and recognize individual growth and achievements.
- ✓ Lead by example: Demonstrate your commitment to continuous learning by pursuing your own development. Share your experiences of learning and growth with your team members, showcasing the value of lifelong learning.
- ✓ Encourage self-reflection: Encourage individuals to reflect on their experiences, successes, and failures. Foster a culture

where individuals can learn from both positive and negative experiences and apply those lessons to future situations.

- ✓ Provide learning opportunities: Provide access to learning resources such as training programs, workshops, conferences, or online courses. Support employees in acquiring new skills and knowledge relevant to their roles and future career aspirations.
- ✓ Encourage curiosity and questioning: Foster a culture of curiosity by encouraging employees to ask questions, challenge assumptions, and seek innovative solutions. Create forums for brainstorming and idea generation, where diverse perspectives are welcomed and explored.
- ✓ Support personal development plans: Collaborate with employees to develop personal development plans that align with their career goals and aspirations. Provide guidance and resources to support their growth, and regularly review and adjust these plans as needed.
- ✓ Emphasize learning from failure: Encourage employees to view failure as an opportunityto learn and grow. Create an environment where individuals feel safe to take risks and learn from their mistakes. Encourage a growth mindset that embraces failures as stepping stones to success and fosters resilience.
- ✓ Establish knowledge-sharing platforms: Implement knowledge-sharing platforms or communities of practice where employees can share their expertise, best practices, and lessons learned. Encourage cross-functional

collaboration and create opportunities for employees to learn from one another's experiences.

✓ Support ongoing professional development: Invest in the professional development of your team members by providing resources for attending conferences, participating in workshops, or obtaining certifications. Encourage employees to pursue continuous learning outside of their immediate job responsibilities.

✓ Regularly assess learning needs: Continuously assess the learning and development needs of your team and organization. Stay informed about industry trends and emerging technologies, and ensure that your employees have the necessary skills and knowledge to adapt to changing demands.

✓ Celebrate learning milestones: Celebrate individual and team learning milestones as an important part of your organizational culture. Recognize and reward employees who actively pursue learning and demonstrate a commitment to personal and professional growth.

✓ Encourage cross-functional exposure: Provide opportunities for employees to gain exposure to different areas of the organization. Encourage job rotations, cross-departmental projects, or mentorship programs that allow individuals to learn from different perspectives and expand their skill sets.

✓ Foster a growth-oriented feedback culture: Promote a culture of feedback and learning by providing regular constructive feedback to your team members. Encourage employees to seek feedback from their peers and provide support and guidance for improvement.

✓ Emphasize the value of continuous improvement: Communicate the importance of continuous improvement as a means to stay competitive and drive organizational success. Celebrate small wins and incremental improvements, and encourage employees to embrace a mindset of constant learning and growth.

By observing how eagles exhibit humility and a mindset of continuous learning, leaders can cultivate these qualities within themselves and their organizations. By valuing the contributions of others, embracing a culture of continuous learning, and encouraging personal and professional development, leaders can foster an environment of growth, innovation, and success.

Conclusion

As we conclude our journey through the pages of **'Eagle-Eyed Leadership: Unleashing the Power of 31 Lessons from Eagles'** we hope you have gained valuable insights and inspiration from the remarkable qualities of eagles. These magnificent creatures have taught us that true leadership is not just about position or authority, but about embodying a set of timeless principles and behaviors.

Throughout this book, we have explored essential lessons that leaders can learn from eagles and apply in their own leadership roles. From vision and focus to adaptability, strategic planning, effective communication, leading by example, teamwork, decision-making, coaching team members, continuous learning, and more, each lesson has illuminated a path to leadership excellence.

Leadership is a continuous journey of growth and development. It requires self-awareness, empathy, and a commitment to continuous improvement. By drawing upon the wisdom of eagles, we have seen how leaders can embrace their unique strengths, foster collaboration, navigate challenges, and inspire their teams to reach new heights.

But our exploration does not end here. The lessons from eagles are not confined to these pages; they live within you. As you close this book, remember that leadership is a daily practice. Embrace the lessons and integrate them into your leadership style. Let them guide your decisions, actions, and interactions with others.

Take the time to reflect on the remarkable qualities of eagles: their vision, adaptability, strategic planning, effective communication, leading by example, teamwork, decision-making, continuous learning, and more. Embrace the values of humility, empathy, and ethical conduct that eagles exemplify. Seek opportunities to inspire and motivate those around you, and foster a culture of collaboration and innovation.

Remember that leadership is not solely about personal success but also about empowering others to thrive. Lift others up, support their growth, and create an environment where everyone can soar to their fullest potential.

We hope that **'Eagle-Eyed Leadership'** has ignited your passion for leadership and provided you with practical tools and inspiration. As you embark on your leadership journey, always keep the spirit of eagles in your heart. Let their remarkable attributes guide you as you lead with purpose, integrity, and a commitment to excellence.

Now is the time to spread your wings, embrace the lessons learned, and soar to new horizons of leadership greatness. As you take flight, remember the lessons from eagles, and may you leave a lasting impact on your teams, organizations, and the world.

So, go ahead, spread your wings and let your leadership soar!

About the Author
'GERARD ASSEY'

Gerard Assey is a Graduate in Economics, a PGD in Management (HRD) and holds a Doctorate in Leadership. Gerard holds several International Qualifications in Sales, Debt Collection, Training & Teaching, and is a 'Fellow' of the prestigious 'Institute of Sales & Marketing Management'-UK, a Certified NLP Practitioner, a 'Certified Trainer', an 'Accredited Management Teacher-Behavioral Sciences', a 'Certified Competency Facilitator', a 'Certified Management Consultant'- (the International credentials of a professional management consultant, awarded in accordance with global standards of the ICMCI); and a Certification from the University of Michigan in 'Successful Negotiation: Essential Strategies and Skills'

He is also a Member of the 'National Association of Sales Professionals' backed with several years experience in varied industries, both in India and Overseas. He also holds an 'Etiquette Consultant' Certification from the USA (by Sue Fox, Author of Best Seller: 'Business Etiquette for Dummies'. She has trained some of the top celebrities' world over). He was also a recipient of a scholarship for extensive training in Japan on 'Corporate Management for India'.

Gerard Assey is 'Founder & Chief Corporate Trainer' of the Group: **Citius, Altius, Fortius Unlimited**'- an organization that **celebrated 20 years of Glorious Service** in 2021, focusing on 3 Core Competencies:

People. Performance. Profit; in functional areas of Sales & Marketing, HR & Organizational Development, covering Recruitment, Training & Consultancy!

Having managed organizations with large Sales Forces in India & Overseas, his specialization cover extensive areas of Sales Training (All levels - Presentation, Negotiation, Key/ Strategic Accounts Management & Managerial Skills for all sectors), Bid Proposal/ Capture Planning/ Management Trainings, Retail Sales, Customer Service & Customer Retention Programs, Training for Prevention & Collection of Debt, Self & Personal Development Programs (Time Management, Teamwork & Team Building, Business Etiquette & Personal Grooming, Leadership & Managerial Skills, People Management Skills, Train-the-Trainer etc), including preparation of Custom-designed Business Manuals for Internal (HR, Induction, and Sales etc) & External use (Instruction, User Manuals).

Gerard has successfully conducted over 6060 Trainings & Workshops (as of Feb '24) all across India, Middle East, Africa, Europe & S.E. Asia. Besides public programs conducted regularly, both in India & Overseas, he has some of the top names as clients whom he services from Single Owners to large Public & Government undertakings, covering all sectors, for their in-house needs.

His website: www.CollectionSkills.com is the only one in this part of the world to be featured in the 'Collections & Credit Risk Magazine-USA' under 'Who's Who in Training' and ranks TOP, along with other websites listed below on most search engines.

Gerard is author of 108 books already (Feb 2024)

A few of our business related books:

1. Bite-sized Bits on Commonsense Management
2. Heart to Heart on Life's Principles'
3. How to become a Successful Manager
4. The Sales Professionals' Master Workbook of S.Y.S.T.E.M.S
5. The Professional Business Email Etiquette Handbook & Guide
6. The Professional Business Video-Conferencing Etiquette Handbook & Guide
7. Professional Presentation Skills
8. Exceptional Customer Service
9. Professional Tele-Marketing Skills
10. Professional Debt Collection Skills
11. The G.R.E.A.T. Sales & Service Workbook
12. Sales Training Advantage for Results (*The Ultimate Sales Training Manual to enable you stand out as a S.T.A.R.*)
13. CEO Daily Planner & Organizer
14. The Sales Professionals' Master Daily Planner
15. The Professional Debt Collector's Master Daily Planner
16. My Daily Planner & Organizer
17. MY EMERGENCY INFORMATION RECORD (Family Emergency & Peace of Mind Planner)
18. The Ultimate Therapist & Counselors Planner and Organizer
19. Building an Ethical Workplace
20. Managing Relationships at Work
21. Managing Business Meetings Effectively
22. Effective Delegation Skills
23. Goal Setting for Success
24. B2B Selling by Email
25. Professional Business Etiquette & Grooming
26. Dining Etiquette & Table Manners
27. Effective Networking Skills
28. Grooming, Etiquette & Manners for Teens, Young Adults & Future Leaders
29. Inter-Personal Skills
30. Get Ready, Get Hired!
31. Selling in a Recession
32. Effective Receivables Management in an Economic Downturn!
33. Real Estate & Property Sales Training

Besides regularly contributing to business & trade journals, including international ones such as the 'Creative Training Techniques' and the 'Sales News' of the U.S.A, He is also a member of several prestigious bodies & trade associations, having participated in many Conferences & Workshops in India & Overseas.

Prior to his last assignment of leading & managing a large MNC as head, Gerard had a 3-year stint in the Middle East as a Consultant with a leading British Consultancy Firm.

As the past 'Official Country Representative' for the International Business Award- 'THE STEVIES'-(the business world's own Oscar) for about 4 years- he ensured a few Indian companies that qualify for the same every year!

Gerard can be contacted at:
Email: training@Sales-Training.in, training@CollectionSkills.com

Websites:

www.Sales-Training.in
www.EtiquetteWorks.in
www.CollectionSkills.com
www.RetailSalesTraining.in
www.SalesTrainingIndia.com
www.ManualPreparation.com
www.TrainingWithPuppets.com
www.FirstContactAcademy.com
www.SalesAndMarketingRecruiter.com

Our TRAININGS that can help your team

- ✓ **Sales Effectiveness**: Selling Skills for any Sector: Service/ Logistics/ FMCG Realty/ Insurance & Finance/ Media/ SPA's, Health Clubs & Salons/ Key Account Management, Effective Negotiation Skills/ Bid & Proposal Management Skills/ Retail Sales Training: Any Sector (Auto, Jewelry, Clothing, Luxury etc)
- ✓ **Customer Service Skills**-Complaints Handling & Customer Retention
- ✓ **Debt Prevention & Collection Skills**
- ✓ **Etiquette & Grooming**
- ✓ **Leadership & Managerial Skills**
- ✓ **Self & Personal Development Skills**: Presentation Skills/ Effective Communication Skills/Business Proposal Writing Skills/ Problem Solving & Decision Making Skills/ Empowering Secretaries-The perfect PA! (For Secretaries & PA's)/ Effective Time Management/ Teamwork & Teambuilding/ P.R.I.D.E- **P**ersonal **R**esponsibility **I**n **D**elivering **E**xcellence